PRAISE FOR

"Jim Afremow's book *The Leader's Mind* clearly demonstrates a vital and eternal truth—so as you think, so shall you be. Believe it!"

—JAMEY ROOTES,
President of the Houston Texans

"In *The Leader's Mind*, Jim Afremow uses a diverse collection of fascinating leaders who represent complex and inspiring insights into the highest levels of leadership thought. Their stories of relationships, empowerment, and vulnerability resonate with all who choose a path to rise above suggestions and conjecture, and lead from the most knowledgeable heart spaces, to 'stay in the game' regardless of any challenges."

—JOANNE P. MCCALLIE,
Former Women's Basketball Coach at Duke
and Michigan State universities, named
National Coach of the Year
by the Associated Press
and *Basketball Times*

"A valuable case study into the DNA of leadership. A roadmap to inspire your team toward authentic enrollment."

—MARK MCLAUGHLIN, MD,
Author of *Cognitive Dominance*

"Jim Afremow and Phil White have hit a home run. The deeply compelling stories of several extraordinary leaders, whose actions and words both inspire and teach, offer concrete lessons for all of us as we embrace the mantra 'leaders are made, not born.'"

—MARC POLYMEROPOULOS,
Fomer CIA Senior Intelligence Officer
and Author of *Clarity in Crisis*

"We are in an era where there is a profound and ongoing need for true leadership on so many fronts. In *The Leader's Mind*, Jim Afremow dissects the essence of leadership down to its bare bones. You will gain a full appreciation of what leadership is, its many faces, and how to recognize truly great leaders, at all levels in life. It may also inspire *you* to lead, ultimately changing your world, or the world."

—NICHOLAS DINUBILE, MD,
Orthopedic Surgeon and Bestselling Author

THE
LEADER'S
MIND

HOW GREAT LEADERS
PREPARE, PERFORM, AND PREVAIL

JIM AFREMOW, PhD
WITH PHIL WHITE

HarperCollins
Leadership

AN IMPRINT OF HarperCollins

Published by HarperCollins Leadership,
an imprint of HarperCollins Focus LLC.

Any internet addresses, phone numbers, or company or product
information printed in this book are offered as a resource and are not
intended in any way to be or to imply an endorsement by HarperCollins
Leadership, nor does HarperCollins Leadership vouch for the existence,
content, or services of these sites, phone numbers, companies, or
products beyond the life of this book.

ISBN 978-1-4002-2576-7 (eBook)
ISBN 978-1-4002-2562-0 (TP)

Library of Congress Control Number: 2021943890

Printed in the United States of America

HB 08.25.2023

To my wife, Anne, and our daughter, Maria Paz,
for their unwavering love and support.
—J.A.

To my wife, Nicole, and sons, Harry and Johnny,
for the editing, encouragement, and putting up with
Daddy being in his office too much.
—P.W.

CONTENTS

INTRODUCTION

Leaders aren't born, they are made. And they are made just like anything else, through hard work. And that's the price we'll have to pay to achieve that goal, or any goal.

—VINCE LOMBARDI

Zen master Ryokan was walking on a beach where many starfish had been scattered during a recent storm and now lay dying in the bright sun. Ryokan picked up starfish and tossed them, one by one, back into the sea.

A nearby fisherman approached Ryokan and asked, "You can't save all the starfish, so what difference does your effort make?"

"It will make a difference to this one," *replied Ryokan, as he cast another starfish into the water.*

—ZEN PARABLE

A legendary coach, a Zen master, and you. What makes a leader? What do leaders do? Are you a leader? Almost by definition, notable leaders inspire a great number of people. It is easy to think that there is a secret sauce that will motivate and inspire others by the thousands. In actuality, while the overall effect reaches many, each inspiration sparks one person at a time. What makes a person think, *Yes, it matters to me, too?*

This contemporary collection of interviews and accounts of outstanding leaders reflects a common thread: The leaders have a clear awareness of how their actions and words impact others, one person at a time. And they each use potent mental skills that help them navigate highs and lows, push through setbacks, and squeeze every last ounce of potential from themselves and the people they serve. In short, they have developed a Leader's Mind. And so can you.

We will learn how leaders nurture their teams, whether comprising firefighters, flight attendants, or doctors and nurses. We will hear from one of the winningest coaches in college sports about how he shapes the trajectory of young lives. And we will learn how a Nazi soldier's unexpected act of kindness inspired an entrepreneur to change the world for the better. To add a framework to several key principles of leadership, we'll talk with leaders who have applied a Stoic philosophy. These tenets will help you to apply battle-tested leadership in your own life, while you make your mindset the most potent tool at your disposal.

In the opening chapter, we meet Nick Peters, a leader who works in the midst of fire, where life and death can come from a miscalculation of wind and terrain. Peters worked his way up from a grunt firefighter to a district fire management officer, leading teams across 305,000 acres of Chattahoochee-Oconee National Forest in northern Georgia. He describes how he got into the minds of his firefighters so that he could get them past the fear of a forest fire bearing down on them at the crest of a hill. Peters talks about what gets him through each day at the "office" and at home, how he deals with decision fatigue, and what he does to keep communication flowing along the fire line.

In Chapter 2, we share the compelling story of Steve Kerr, from his humble beginnings as a lightly recruited college player who worked his way into legendary Arizona Wildcats basketball coach Lute Olson's rotation and earned a spot on a Team USA World Championship squad. We'll explore how

Kerr displayed grace following his father's untimely death and developed grit and determination to outplay his doubters' expectations, bounce back from a serious knee injury, and make it into the NBA. In the next stage of Kerr's journey, we'll see what he picked up from teammates like Michael Jordan and all-time coaching greats Phil Jackson and Gregg Popovich, on the way to winning five titles. Kerr's career then took a detour into television commentary and serving as general manager for the Phoenix Suns. We'll learn how these experiences and his friendship with the Seattle Seahawks' Super Bowl-winning coach Pete Carroll prepared Kerr to transform the Golden State Warriors from contenders into champions with a core values–based leadership approach.

In Chapter 3, we meet pilot Tammie Jo Shults. As the captain of Southwest Airlines flight 1380, Shults took control of the plane when an uncontained engine failure threw debris to the fuselage, causing damage, depressurization, and the tragic death of a passenger who was partially ejected.

How many leaders experience such a moment, when the fate of hundreds is in their hands? How would most react? What does one draw upon to do what needs to be done? Shults talks about this incident and what she does routinely for each and every flight to get the best out of her crew and ensure the utmost safety for passengers. She also shares how she overcame gender bias as a pioneering US Navy pilot and the principles that guide her decision-making in the air and on the ground.

In Chapter 4, we go behind the scenes of the most successful team in sports history, the mighty New Zealand All Blacks, through the eyes of the team's longtime strength and conditioning coach, Nic Gill.[1] Other books have offered third-party observations about the team's leadership principles, dedication to continued excellence, and relentlessly self-improving mindset; but none deliver the true insider's view that Gill provides. He shares the secrets of practicing presence on the road and at home with his family, the lessons in on-field leadership he learned from rugby legends Richie McCaw and Steve Hansen, and the true key to the All Blacks' unique culture. Gill reveals how he and the team he serves remain supremely confident yet humble. He also discusses techniques for embracing high expectations and the best way to bounce back from an unexpected and crushing defeat.

What kind of leader do you respect? What kind of leader are you? What kind of leader do you want to become? In Chapter 5, we meet neurosurgeon Katrina Firlik. We hear from her what it means to hold life and death in your palms, and how, even for this superbly skilled professional, there is a thrill in being part of a team. She emphasizes the importance of lifelong learning and how leadership comes from knowing yourself. Firlik also explains how she mentally approached a significant mid-career pivot, the operating room lessons she learned from an experienced mentor, and how she kept her concentration and composure in one of the most high-pressured branches of modern medicine.

Paul Ratcliffe is a highly successful coach with a proven track record at one of the most competitive and prestigious universities in the world. Chapter 6 reviews how, almost unbelievably, he has led his Stanford team to the NCAA tournament every season. Coaches help to shape the attitude, actions, and mindset of young people at a formative time in their lives. They inspire, motivate, and move their teams forward, creating the next generation of leaders.

Is leadership an innate gift? Is it acquired through training in an MBA program or ROTC? Is it something we can develop in ourselves? Ratcliffe reflects on the humble origins of what he sees as true leadership.

In Chapter 7, we hear about several key principles from Stoic philosophy in interviews with psychotherapist Donald Robertson. First and foremost, he said, one should have a goal in life. Instead of just going through the motions or tackling life's daily problems one at a time, there should be a larger aim. Next, he describes several potent Stoic strategies to help you move constantly toward this goal. Many of these can also be thought of as psychological tactics, such as reframing a negative situation into a welcome challenge, acknowledging an insult but choosing to ignore it, and noting some anger, anxiety, or envy but not acting on it. Putting such ancient wisdom into practice requires use and repetition, like training for a sport. As I often tell leaders, mental skills are not magic skills and must be cultivated daily. As a Stoic, you will be in constant training, ready to flex your mindset muscles, and rising to the occasion when the time comes.

In our eighth and final chapter, we discover the significance of mission-driven leadership in the life of entrepreneur Daniel Lubetzky. His story has its roots in the horrors of the Holocaust, where his father, Roman, found that even in the barren soil of great evil and suffering, the flower of human kindness can flourish. This chapter reveals the significance of the stories Lubetzky heard at his father's feet and how they informed his mission to enable reconciliation in the war-torn Middle East. We also follow Lubetzky as he lugs a heavy suitcase of samples through the streets of New York day after day, and how this persistence resulted in a business breakthrough. Finally, we learn how—even after KIND Bar went from a small, start-up enterprise to a billion-dollar-plus company—philanthropy, optimism, and principled leadership remain at the heart of Lubetzky's career and legacy.

This book presents a unique panel of leaders from many walks of life and from various industries and professions. You will certainly find a leader and a leadership style that speak to your background and aspirations. There are also a bevy of mindset tips, tools, and techniques in the coming pages that you can apply to elevate your own leadership skills, no matter what game day means to you. Don't consider yourself a leader? Think about all the roles you play in life, and I bet you'll find a way in which you are leading or could grow into a leadership position. It could be in your job, your vocation, your home, or your community. I believe there is a leader in you, and I hope that the pages you're holding in your hands help you become a great one.

No other book on leadership takes you from a raging inferno to the sterile chill of a surgical theater to the fervor of a Rugby World Cup final. In these firsthand accounts, you'll glimpse how highly skilled professionals handled formative moments in their careers, embraced struggle, and fueled their enduring commitment to develop the people they lead. You'll also see real-life examples of how leaders employ skills such as self-talk, mental toughness, and confidence to great effect. Lastly, and importantly, the overview of Stoicism provides a way to apply a time-tested philosophy to your life and the way you lead others.

There are many roads to leadership. It's time to embark on your own journey toward developing a Leader's Mind.

CHAPTER 1

LEADERSHIP UNDER FIRE

Leadership can be summed up as just be a good person.

—NICK PETERS, *District Fire Management Officer, United States Forest Service*

How many of our leaders must perform at their best when death can come in an instant with a simple miscalculation of wind and terrain? Nick Peters is such a leader, having worked his way up from a grunt firefighter to a district fire management officer, leading teams across 305,000 acres of the Chattahoochee-Oconee National Forest in northern Georgia. Here is how he describes one situation in which he found himself:

> I was already in place and the crew boss was nowhere around, so I grabbed a half dozen people and said, "Let's go, we've got to burn this thing out." As we're going, we were working just off the top of this ridge, and, as you know, fire runs uphill, then it goes downhill. The fire was coming up one side. We were just on the backside of this ridge, and we had to burn out the ridge. The containment line was down below us, maybe a hundred yards to a road. I had these firefighters, and a bunch of them were new.
>
> They had never been in that part of the country on that big of a fire. As we were moving forward, the

fire started cresting the top, and we're talking fifty- to hundred-foot flames, within fifty feet of us. Because fire goes uphill and goes up in altitude, we weren't feeling the heat from it, but it was right there, and it was roaring fire, and all these kids froze.

But we had to get the job done. I knew we were good, and we could outrun the fire downhill if necessary, but all these guys were frozen solid. At one point, I had to look at them and say: "Hey, snap out of it! We got a job to do. Follow me. Do as I tell you to do."

His example has much to offer in terms of its application to leadership. In an interview for this book, Peters shares with us several key concepts and techniques, including: "Living an Adventure," "Life Is Communication," "What You Can't Control," "The Observe, Orient, Decide, and Act (OODA) Loop," "It's All About Values," "Trigger Points," "After Action Review," and "Attitude: I Still Have a Roof over My Head."

In this chapter, we'll learn from Nick Peters as he offers several important concepts along with key values and practical techniques to apply to teams, colleagues, and your own leadership. (These are the personal views of Nick Peters and do not necessarily represent those of the USDA US Forest Service.)

LIVING AN ADVENTURE

Peters found his way to forestry because he was looking for adventure. It's evident that he continues to live that adventure each day. His excitement and pride are palpable as he describes the particulars of his work:

As the district fire management officer, I am responsible for all fire operations that happen in this area. My district is about 305,000 acres. I have a full-time fire engine crew with a small fire engine. Some people call it a brush truck. We base it off of types, and each type is a size. A Type 1 engine would be what you'd see a structure fire crew having. A Type 3 engine would be a pretty large brush truck for out West. And then we have what's called a Type 6 engine, which is a smaller package for being able to get back into the woods a little easier. It carries only three hundred gallons of water.

I've got the engine crew and an operator who is responsible for the dozer and various other equipment. We call our staff and secondary fire personnel our *militia.* Our recreation, timber, and wildlife people also have fire qualifications, and they help us out with wildfires and prescribed burns. Wildfires could be anything from a lightning strike to somebody tossing the ashes from their fireplace and catching the woods on fire, all the way up to arson. Prescribed burning is where we actually go out and put fire on the landscape to restore the forest. Because, as we know, fire is a natural part of the ecosystem.

I started applying for fire jobs because I wanted to live an adventure; I wanted to go do something. I ended up getting hired on in Happy Camp (California) for my first job in 2004. Since then, I've been on engine crews, hand crews, and one season I spent on a helicopter crew where we actually rappelled out of the helicopter into forest fires. That was a really cool job, by the way.

As a leader, what is your adventure? Take a few moments to reflect upon your personal, academic, or career journey so far. How did it start out? By simply listening to your parents? Or maybe you followed a set academic path. Did you start your career in a job that interested you? Did you land an internship just by chance? Did you have a vision or passion that seemed to guide you toward opportunities? Did opportunity present itself because you shared and communicated your aspirations to others, who then helped you move along your path? How have your approach and attitude toward leadership developed over time?

LIFE IS COMMUNICATION

In the US Forest Service, people often travel around the country, going from one job to another. Peters worked at the Wayne National Forest in Ohio, then the Kaibab National Forest in northern Arizona, then on to Oklahoma and Georgia. While moving around can keep things fresh and exciting, there is no denying that it is stressful. Dealing with stress and potential conflict is to be expected in leadership positions. Peters makes it clear: communication is life.

When dealing with a move, a lot of it—especially if you have a spouse involved—is communication. That's the biggest thing with anything we do in life. I'm not going to tell my wife: "Hey, guess what? We're moving to the middle of nowhere in Nevada. Hope you enjoy it," even though my wife did tell me, "I'll follow you wherever you want to go." I took her to western

Oklahoma, and that was not the greatest of places. But as long as you have that open communication and the support of your spouse, you can accomplish anything.

Probably one of the greatest orators in US history was President Abraham Lincoln. How many of us have memorized parts of his Gettysburg Address? President Ronald Reagan was known as the Great Communicator, because he knew how to speak to Americans. When leaders communicate, they transform their audiences into one body that is greater than the sum of its parts.

WHAT YOU CAN'T CONTROL

Many see leadership as a decision-making role. We've all heard of alpha males making top-down "executive decisions." While certainly this is true in many situations, realize that the flip side of decision making is a situation where one has very little control. Imagine being Nick Peters in the midst of a fire. What variables are outside of his control? The wind, weather, and equipment failures, just to name a few. Imagine the stress of trying to protect homes, personal property, forest, and lives as countless variables swirl around uncontrollably.

A lot of that boils down to stress management and knowing what you have control of and knowing what you don't have control of. Is there a way you can take control of the things that you don't have control of? If not, then you let them go.

Peters sees stress as a human construction and recognizes that there are some things you can change and some things that you can't. Most important, he reflects on something that leaders can concentrate on: the emotional and physical toll of stress. What are his techniques for recovering and bouncing back strong after being on a big burn for days and sometimes even weeks on end?

One of the hardest parts of my job right now is that I'm no longer digging the line to actively stop the fire. Now I'm managing and directing the firefighters who are doing that on the ground. I'm out there in the field with them all day long, supervising, making sure that they're doing the work, that it's timely, that we're going to be able to meet our objectives, and that everybody goes home at the end of the day. With that comes a lot of critical decision making.

The last fire that I was on, it seemed like every twenty minutes we were adapting our plans, sometimes because the weather or the fire changed so our initial plan wasn't going to work anymore. So, I had to make new decisions and relay them to everyone on the line. That constant decision making, especially in a time-critical, highly dynamic environment, is extremely fatiguing.

After that fire, I told my wife, "I'm not making a decision for three days." That was my way of countering the mental fatigue of a constant decision-making matrix. When I got home, I didn't care what we ate, I didn't care where we went, I didn't care what we did.

Just because of mental fatigue, I didn't make a single decision. As far as physical fatigue, we do a lot of physical training. I think I heard somebody refer to wildland firefighters as tactical athletes. Every morning we're in the gym, and by 6:00 a.m., we're working out, whether it be running, lifting weights, whatever. We're working on our physical fitness because our bodies need it for what we do. This makes recovery that much easier when we get home and we're totally physically drained. A couple days of relaxation, and we're ready to go.

THE OBSERVE, ORIENT, DECIDE, AND ACT (OODA) LOOP

Peters uses the OODA loop to structure and facilitate his decision making. Such conceptual tools are important to apply and can help to work through a precarious, stressful, and urgent situation, as he explains:

> The OODA loop was developed by John Boyd, who was a military aviator. He said that the fighter pilot who could go through the OODA loop the fastest is the one who wins dogfights. OODA is an acronym for *observe, orient, decide, and then act.* You're making an observation of your overall surroundings. You're then orienting yourself to that. Next, you make a decision based on your situational awareness, what you've just obtained, and act upon it. Then you immediately go right back into the observation phase.
>
> The great thing about the OODA loop is that it breaks out the bias of split-second decisions. It allows

you to be in the moment on a specific task, and, at the same time, to focus on the big picture. We use it within our agency as a decision-making tool. It works very well with just cutting through the BS, looking at what is really going on. What's happening? Why is it going on? Where are you involved in it? What is the task at hand? What are our overall objectives? How do we get to our mission results?

We make a decision based on this information, act on it, and then reevaluate. Then we go right back into the observe phase and ask, "Are we meeting the objectives? Are we going to make our deadline? Are the jobs that we're doing out in the field going be successful or not?" If they're not going to be successful, we have to reevaluate, because in the end, we're trying to find the highest likelihood of success. The number one priority is that everybody goes home. Number two, we put the fire out.

As a leader, what decision-making tools do you typically employ? What concepts or steps help you to break through the fog of an emotionally charged situation? Do you even activate physical circuit breakers such as pausing for a count of three or ten before responding? Are you able to reset a situation to remove some of the political or personal conflicts that can prevent things from moving forward on a rational tack? Peters's approach, he said, is to help bring people back to the mission and policies:

I would resort to our standard operating procedures, to our core beliefs in firefighting and in leadership. Those are duty, integrity, and respect. These are ingrained in every single one of us from the beginning. If an individual is outside of those realms, if they're not respecting their coworkers or aren't following their duty, or have less integrity, I resort to these three values. I won't make the problem between me and an individual. I'll fall back on our standard operating procedures, our protocols and procedures, and make it about those. That's what we are supposed to be following and adhering to.

If an individual is bullying, that's not being respectful toward others. I would pull them into my office and say: "Look, I have witnessed this going on, and you know that our standard operating procedures are duty, integrity, and respect. Please explain to me how you felt this action was respectful toward others." Then I've completely eliminated myself from the problem, and I've resorted to our policy.

IT'S ALL ABOUT VALUES

Contemporary leadership principles and corporate policies are constantly promoting values. While corporations often fall short, it is still crucial that a person holds particular values close to heart. According to Peters:

The key principles of duty, integrity, and respect help build a better, more resilient US Forest Service. Duty is being proficient in your job, technically and as a leader. Your duty is to make sound and timely decisions, ensure tactics are understood, supervised, and accomplished. My duty as a leader is to make sure that everybody's doing their job and doing it safely and accurately. Another part of leadership is developing others to bring them up in the future. Because I wouldn't be where I am if it wasn't for people along the way who have mentored and guided me, and steered me in the direction that led me here. If I don't do the same thing for the people who work for me, I am doing a disservice to them.

It's amazing that you actually have to explain to some people what respect really looks like. To me, it's knowing your subordinates and looking out for their well-being, keeping my subordinates informed. I can't tell you how many supervisors I've had who didn't do that. They thought information was power, and so they held onto it. Well, information isn't power if you hold onto it. Information is power when everybody knows it.

The core of leadership is building your team to be a stronger, more resilient, functioning group. And then utilizing employer subordinates in accordance with their capabilities. Obviously, I'm not going to have my first-year rookie firefighters grab a chainsaw and cut the most dangerous tree out there. That's not setting them up for success. That's actually setting them up for failure. And it could be extrapolated down to even the smallest tasks.

I'm going to make sure that I employ my people in the best capability for their safety, for everybody's safety around them, and also in a way that will help them develop and grow. My captain, for instance, is not a high-complexity sawyer. He's a moderate-complexity sawyer, but he's on the verge of being a high-complexity sawyer. I can put him on a really tough, tricky tree as long as I'm right there next to him, guiding him and mentoring him.

Our last leadership value is integrity. Leadership can be summed up as simply as "Just be a good person." As long as you're a good person, you're looking out for everybody's well-being, you want to promote everyone, and you want to give everybody the opportunity for success and development. That right there is integrity: know yourself and seek improvement. You need to be humble in leadership and in anything you do. If you go into it thinking, *I know everything*, you're missing something, and you're going to start developing poor habits.

Another part of integrity is seeking and accepting responsibility for your actions. We've all seen the individual who passes blame onto others. In my district with my crew, even if one of my guys does something that he shouldn't have done, that's my responsibility because it was my job to make sure that everything is done according to policy and procedure. So, that's on me; I hold that. If it's a failure, that's my responsibility. If it's a success, I can't take credit for everybody else. I have to pass that success on because they're the ones who did the work, not me.

The last thing with integrity is setting an example. That goes back to being a good person. It's amazing how many people think they're a good leader, but they're not a good person. And if you think back to all the good and bad leaders that you've witnessed in your life, it's the ones who were not a good person that really stand out. When you ask yourself, "What kind of leader do I want to be?" are you really going to look at the individual who is not a good person and say, "I want to be like that person"? Not likely.

As a leader, what are your key values? Are they reflected in your corporate policies? Your clubhouse bylaws? Your team dynamics? How do you apply your values at home, among friends, and to family?

TRIGGER POINTS

Once we have enough experience in a particular field, we arrive at a point where much of what we do comes as second nature. However, it is often important to provide "checks" on our more emotional selves. For example, pilots go through a lengthy preflight checklist where they review one item at a time, back and forth, to ensure safety. In the operating room, current practice nowadays involves the simple act of writing "left" or "right" on an arm or leg to ensure that you're working on the appropriate limb. Nick Peters is no different. Here he describes triggers that he checks in the midst of a wildfire:

Once you do this long enough, a lot of it becomes second nature. When the winds start picking up, for instance, everybody knows that the fire can become erratic. It might change direction. Maybe there's a cold front coming in, and you're going to potentially have strong gusty winds. These might turn erratic, which means the fire could blow in any direction. So, the minute the wind starts picking up, if you start noticing that, we call it a *trigger point*.

Once that trigger point is hit, you say: "Okay, hold on, time out. Let's reevaluate. Are we still going to be able to meet those objectives? Are we still going to be able to complete our mission safely?" And that goes back to what I mentioned before about the OODA loop. Any time there's a change in the environment, you immediately go right back into that observation stage and reevaluate the mission, where you are within it, and whether you can accomplish it. And if not, let's change the task to see if we can meet the mission objectives with a different approach.

What other people might see as multiple changes within the environment can be simplified as important trigger points. If the winds get up over twenty miles an hour, let's stop and reevaluate. If our humidity drops below 20 percent—or 15 percent or 10 percent, depending on where you are—let's stop and reevaluate. If our temperatures start rising and we get to ninety or one hundred degrees—whatever those critical thresholds are, once you hit that point, you stop and reevaluate.

Another thing that we're taught early on in our fire careers is the notion of taking ten at two. If you look back at all of the fatal fires that have happened over the course of history, 90 percent of them have occurred between the hours of two and four o'clock in the afternoon. That's when it's the hottest, that's when it's the driest. And so we take a ten-minute break at two o'clock every day. That's going to make sure that we stop and take a look at our surroundings. Because if you're just constantly in the motion of the operation, your head's down, you're digging dirt, you're not paying attention to your surroundings. So, that forces everybody to take a break, look at the big picture, and ask: "Are we good to go? Okay, let's go."

In your daily work or maybe even in your personal life, have you identified some key triggers that can help you notice, adapt to, and engage a change in circumstances? Without such built-in triggers, you may be susceptible to shifts in the wind rather than being able to pivot and apply a more efficient strategy.

AFTER ACTION REVIEWS

The After Action Review (AAR) is a technique that is used in many fields. It may be known as a debrief, a postmortem, or an audit. Whatever the name, progress often involves looking at what worked, what didn't, and trying to learn a bit from history, as Peters describes:

An After Action Review is something that we do regularly. It could be daily, it could be based on a week of work if we have a big operation, a lot of moving pieces—whether we're doing a big burnout operation or a big structure protection. If the fire is slow, mundane, and a long way out, we're just doing a lot of prep work along roads, getting our piece of ground ready to receive that fire, so, I'm going to ask everybody to come together to do an AAR right away. Or I may wait and have a few days before we have another one.

Our AARs are very simple. There are four questions: What was planned? What actually happened? Why did it happen? And what can we do next time? Right there, we are self-evaluating our operation. We're constantly critiquing ourselves—we don't point fingers, we don't name names, we keep it constructive. We want to know if there is anything that we could have done differently to increase our odds of success.

As a leader performing an AAR, how can you be sure you hear from every voice in the room? In some studies, researchers have found that the simple gaze of a leader on a meeting participant can either encourage or discourage communication.[1] Peters sees this, too:

We try to keep it as rankless as possible. My AARs that I tend to lead, I bring everybody into the fold. We could have two hundred people in a circle. I will find a first- or second-year firefighter to lead that After Action Review. That gives someone the opportunity to start working on command presence and communication skills in a big group. If you want to have a career in wildland fire, at some point you're going to have to lead a briefing with people. You need to start getting comfortable with talking in front of groups of people.

Usually it's at the end of the day. Everybody's exhausted from working, and sometimes you don't get a whole lot of feedback. If there are a lot of folks who just want to get things off their chest, then we might have excessive dialogue. But either way, I'm going to try to poke and prod and get people to talk if nobody's talking. If people are talking, I'm just going to let it go. As long as it's constructive, let's have the conversation, because I don't want anybody thinking, *He didn't care what I thought.* That's not my intent. I want to make sure that every voice is heard all the way down to the first-year firefighter. If you see something, say something. Because we can all learn from it.

ATTITUDE: I STILL HAVE A ROOF OVER MY HEAD

The final concept Peters discussed during our interview is one that is useful at work, at home, or anywhere in the world: maintain a positive attitude by holding on to a healthy perspective.

Attitude is so contagious, whether it's positive or negative. It's like a cancer when it's negative. It can completely crumble a program, a group, and an entire work environment. It can bring it to its knees.

Positive attitude can have the exact opposite effect. You can choose to have the best attitude every single day. It can put things back into perspective. So, a job that we were planning on doing got canceled, or we put in a lot of work toward something and it was all for nothing. Guess what? I still have a roof over my head. I still have good food in my belly. I have a nice glass of bourbon next to me.

If you key in on the little things, your attitude just came up a little bit, because the situation you're facing isn't as bad as you think it is.

I made it a mental mission of mine that, from here on out, no matter how terrible life is, no matter how shitty the world is, I am going to have the most positive, highest-energy attitude of anybody in the room. If you can control that, you've got it beat. You can control the world.[2]

SUMMARY

This chapter presents leadership principles and techniques from a leader who literally fights fires in his daily work. Nick Peters shared his journey, which for him began as an adventure and continues to present new challenges and shifting winds. The principles include communicating, letting go of what you can't control, holding on to key values, and having the right attitude. Specific tools for the toolbox include the OODA loop, trigger points, and an After Action Review.

CHAPTER 2

THE SHARPSHOOTER

It should be about the players. As soon as the coach becomes the one in the spotlight, you know you're headed for trouble.

—STEVE KERR, *Head Coach, Golden State Warriors*

When thinking about Steve Kerr, it's easy to conjure up an image of the legendary head coach holding aloft one of the three championship trophies that he won with Steph Curry and company. Or to recall the iconic, game-winning shot he drilled after a rare, last-second pass from Michael Jordan to lift the Bulls to victory over the Utah Jazz in Game 6 of the 1997 NBA Finals. Few imagine that under his smooth, easy-smiling surface bubbles a fire forged in the furnace of adversity.

Kerr earned five NBA championship rings as a sharp-shooting player—three with the Chicago Bulls and two with the San Antonio Spurs—and then claimed another three as head coach of the Warriors. He was born in Beirut, Lebanon, where his philanthropist grandfather, Stanley, settled after serving survivors of the Armenian Genocide and helping women and children affected by atrocities in Aleppo and Marash (now known as Kahramanmarash). Though Kerr eventually graduated from Palisades High School in Los Angeles, he got his early education at Cairo American College in Egypt and the American Community School Beirut. His father, Malcolm, served as a professor at ACS Beirut before becoming president of the American University of Beirut.

Topping out at six feet three inches (which may include socks), Kerr was an effective if undersized combo guard for Palisades. Like Steph Curry, the gunner whom Kerr would guide to back-to-back NBA MVP awards, Kerr's relative smallness and lack of elite athleticism meant that he passed under the radar of many college coaches. However, one saw something special in the blond, blue-eyed competitor. Soon enough, Kerr was leaving Los Angeles for Tucson to play for future Hall of Famer Lute Olson's University of Arizona.

Most of the Wildcats' rabid fans had no idea who this unheralded freshman was, but Kerr's efficient shooting and steady ballhandling soon gained their appreciation and repaid Olson's trust.

But bad news was waiting just around the corner. As Kerr's father walked down the hallway to his office at the American University of Beirut, he was gunned down by two armed men who had stormed into the building. Coach Olson and his wife invited the devastated young man into their home to get him through the early stages of grief. Showing a steely resolve, Kerr was back on the court less than a week later.

By the time the spring of 1986 rolled around, Kerr's solid play made him a worthy addition to Team USA for the FIBA World Championship. It was the last time that the national men's team comprised solely amateurs, in this case, only college players. It was a dramatic contrast to the Dream Team six years later—which boasted a world-class lineup including Larry Bird, Magic Johnson, and, unbeknownst to Kerr, his future teammate Michael Jordan. While teammates such as

Kerr's Arizona cohort Sean Elliott, future NBA champion David Robinson, and Kenny "the Jet" Smith (whom Kerr would join as an announcer on TNT many years later) got all the headlines, Kerr continued to do what he'd done best at Arizona, sniping away from long range and taking care of ballhandling duties in the backcourt.

In the semifinals, however, disaster struck. Kerr adjusted in midair to attempt a pass just as a Brazilian defender switched positions at the last second. Landing awkwardly, he felt his right leg twist and then snap underneath him. Though his team would go on to capture the gold medal, the torn ACL and MCL didn't just signal the end of Kerr's tournament, but also his senior season.

With one year of eligibility left, Kerr refused to let the injury keep him down. Battling back after a yearlong rehab, he had his breakout season in 1987–1988 alongside emerging star Sean Elliott. Both were named All-American as they led Arizona to the Final Four, with Kerr setting the NCAA record for three-point field goal accuracy at 57.3 percent and drawing shouts of "Steeeve Kerrr" from the announcers and frenzied Wildcats fans every time he drilled a triple.

LEADERSHIP REFLECTIONS

- What was the biggest life lesson you learned from someone who has passed away?

- When have you been underestimated, and how did you respond?

- Name a big personal or professional obstacle and think about how you overcame it.

INTO THE BIG LEAGUE

Kerr's NBA career commenced in the same way as his collegiate one: underestimated by the public and press. He wouldn't have it any other way. When you get selected in the second round with the fiftieth pick, as Kerr did by the Phoenix Suns in the 1988 draft, nobody sees you coming. So, unlike the blue chip rookies Danny Manning, Rik Smits, and Kerr's FIBA World Championship teammate Charles Smith, who went 1–2–3 in the draft, he was able to fly under the radar for his first few years in the league. After one year in Phoenix, Kerr was traded to the Cleveland Cavaliers, where he spent three seasons before playing briefly for the Orlando Magic. Though he never averaged more than 6.6 points or 17.6 minutes per game during this spell, Kerr's sharpshooting, locker-room presence, and coach-on-the-floor savvy was enough to keep him in the league.

Just when it looked like he was destined to become an NBA journeyman, the Chicago Bulls came calling and Kerr was off to the Windy City. At this point, the team still had All-Star Scottie Pippen, legendary coach Phil Jackson, and a cast of solid veterans, but Michael Jordan had retired to go play baseball in the wake of his father's murder. So, although the Bulls were the defending champions coming off the back of a three-peat, they ended up losing a grueling, seven-game series to their nemesis, the New York Knicks.

The Bulls weren't used to losing, but they did their fair share of it in the first half of the following season, going into the All-Star weekend with a middling 23–25 record. However, two words from Jordan on March 3, 1995, changed everything for Kerr and his teammates: "I'm back."

Following the return of His Airness, the Bulls won twenty-four of their final thirty-four games to make the playoffs, and then crushed the Charlotte Hornets 3–1 in the first round.

However, with Jordan still getting back his feel for the game, they lost to the Orlando Magic's dynamic duo of Shaquille O'Neal and Penny Hardaway in the second round.

NEVER BACK DOWN

Normal service was resumed the next year, with Jordan leading the league in scoring, reeling off forty-four straight wins, and posting the best single-season record, 72–10, in NBA history (although a plucky little club from Northern California would eventually break it; more on this in a moment). Their unprecedented success didn't come without turmoil, though. Early in the Bulls' training camp in the fall of 1995, the famously intense Jordan was pushing his teammates hard in practice. During a scrimmage, he and Kerr started talking trash to each other, and insults soon escalated into blows.[1]

"I took exception to something he said," Kerr recounted later. "So I was talking back and I don't think Michael appreciated that . . . and we got in the lane and he gave me a forearm shiver to the chest and I pushed him back. And next thing you know, our teammates were pulling him off of me." Though he ended up with a black eye, Kerr got a couple of punches of his own in, according to his teammates. Jordan called him later that day to apologize, and both players developed a newfound respect for each other. "It was a totally different relationship from that point on," Kerr said.[2] It wouldn't be long before the trust between Jordan and Kerr would face the ultimate test.

Making the most of their opportunity, the Bulls then beat the Seattle Supersonics, four games to two, to win the NBA title. Kerr had an outstanding season as well, becoming part of the NBA's exclusive "50-40-90" club (shooting 50 percent on two-pointers, 40 percent on three-pointers, and 90 percent at the free-throw line), which includes Larry Bird, Dirk Nowitzki, and two players Kerr would get to know well: Kevin Durant and Steph Curry. Indeed, Kerr was in rare company as a shooter.[3]

I OWE HIM EVERYTHING

The next year, Phil Jackson challenged the team to win back-to-back titles. In their way stood a talented Utah Jazz team led by future Hall of Famers John Stockton and Karl Malone. With the NBA championship and his team's second title of what would be another three-peat on the line, everyone expected Michael Jordan to take and make the winning shot in Game 6. But when John Stockton came over to double-team Jordan, he passed to a wide-open Kerr, who did what he'd done his entire basketball career (including the All-Star Game three-point contest earlier that season, which he won): he nonchalantly knocked down the three-pointer. Game over. Legacy secured.

Afterward, Kerr recounted to the NBA press corps his brief conversation with Jordan in the huddle. "He said, 'You be ready. Stockton is going to come off you.' I said, 'I'll be ready; I'll knock it down.'" Many players would have used this moment for self-aggrandizing, but in typical fashion, Kerr turned the spotlight back on Jordan. "He's so good that he draws so much attention, and his excellence gave me the chance to hit the game-winning shot in the NBA Finals," he said. "What a thrill. I owe him everything."[4]

Heading into the 1997–1998 campaign, the Bulls didn't quite hit the record-setting heights that they'd achieved the year before. But they still posted a 62–20 record, good enough to win the Central Division and finish atop the Eastern Conference standings. Surviving a scare as Reggie Miller and his indefatigable Indiana Pacers took them to seven games, the Bulls battled back into the Finals, where a familiar opponent awaited them: the Utah Jazz. It was Kerr's time to shine again in the final minute of Game 2. Though he missed a three-pointer, he snatched the rebound and passed to Jordan, who converted a three-point play to seal the win. The G.O.A.T. (greatest of all time) then created one of the indelible moments in NBA history in Game 6, crossing over Byron Russell and hitting a trademark fadeaway jumper to clinch the Bulls' second three-peat.

LEADERSHIP REFLECTIONS

- What can you do to be ready to seize the moment when a career-changing opportunity comes along?

- Which leader made a lasting impression on you, and what are the top three lessons you learned from that person?

- How can you apply the example of Jordan and Kerr to better use your team's talents?

FROM THE ZEN MASTER TO POP

With Jordan's retirement and Phil Jackson, Scottie Pippen, Dennis Rodman, and more moving on, the Bulls' dynasty was over. Kerr stayed one more season in Chicago and was then acquired by the San Antonio Spurs. Though the Bulls were all-time greats, the Spurs were no slouches. In addition to adding one of the most NBA-ready rookies in the 1997 draft in Tim Duncan, they had a core of talented veterans, including 1995 MVP David Robinson and Kerr's old Arizona teammate Sean Elliott. This was enough to lift them to the NBA title in the lockout-shortened season before Kerr arrived in Texas.

Another factor that made Kerr eager to sign with the Spurs was their coach. Though prickly in interviews, Gregg Popovich would prove to be one of the game's greats and, Kerr was soon to learn, was far more compassionate with his players than his gruff demeanor suggested.

Popovich would go on to lead the Spurs to five titles and amass more than a thousand wins. But when Kerr joined the team, Popovich was still learning his craft, having only been appointed as head coach two years earlier. Still, Kerr saw his greatness extended beyond the hardwood.

"Pop wasn't Pop yet," Kerr said. "He was a young coach. I didn't know what to expect. But I liked him immediately on a personal level. He was a straight shooter."[5]

The feeling was mutual. Popovich immediately turned to his newly acquired sharpshooter for veteran leadership in the locker room and on the court. During his first few weeks with the Spurs, Kerr came to see that the organization was a family first and a team second. While they had very different personalities, Popovich was creating a similar culture to the one Lute Olson had established at Arizona.

"I just wanted to know that the coach cared about my life and my existence beyond whether I made a shot or not," Kerr said. "That was the first quality that stood out. He wanted to know about my life, my background, my family, my kids."[6]

Once the team got on the practice court, though, it was all business. Kerr was surprised by the way that Popovich yelled at some of his star players, though he noted that those singled out for a drill-sergeant-style dressing-down responded positively and played harder and smarter afterward. Popovich knew how to pick and choose his teaching moments; he could adapt his style to players' different personalities.

"If he had yelled at me, it might have destroyed me," Kerr said. "Because I wasn't a very confident player. I had struggled coming from Chicago to a new system. I didn't play well. Pop was very wise. He knew guys like me, we weren't the right target. You've got to know your audience. You've got to know your team."[7]

LEADERSHIP REFLECTIONS

- How can you show your team members that you care about them?

- Who is an up-and-coming leader you identify with, and what can you learn from that person?

- What can you do better to tailor your communication style to each person you lead?

BACK IN THE VALLEY OF THE SUN

After helping San Antonio knock off their archrivals, the
Dallas Mavericks, with four second-half triples in the 2003
Western Conference Finals, Kerr was a solid backup for Tony
Parker as San Antonio defeated the New Jersey Nets 4–2.
After Game 6, Kerr called time on his playing career, which,
with this latest triumph, ended with five titles and the record
for single-season three-point shooting accuracy (.524, a mark
broken only by Kyle Korver).

Kerr certainly didn't lack options for what to do next. He
opted to join legendary announcer Marv Albert on the NBA
commentary team at TNT. As well as providing insights
on game action, Kerr also shared interesting NBA facts in a
sponsored segment called *Steve's Refreshing Thoughts* that
soon became a viewer favorite.

While continuing his TNT role in 2004, Kerr joined a
group of buyers that purchased the Phoenix Suns. At first,
he was just a consultant for the team, but in June 2007, he
was named general manager. Kerr took over the team during a transition period. During the 2004–2005 season, the
creative mind of coach Mike D'Antoni had created an almost
unguardable, fast-paced offense centered around the talents
of Steve Nash. The team reached the Western Conference
Finals and narrowly lost to the Spurs. The following season,
the Suns overcame Amar'e Stoudemire's knee injuries to
make it back to the final round in the West, where they fell
to Nash's old team, the Mavericks. Nash led the league in
assists and won his second straight MVP award. The next
season was their third in a row winning sixty games or more,

but they again failed to make it past the Spurs, who went on to win the title.

By the time Kerr took over as general manager, Phoenix's glory days were over. To avoid a luxury tax penalty, they traded All-Star forward Shawn Marion for Shaquille O'Neal, who was in the twilight of his illustrious career. Trading for former All-Star Grant Hill was one of Kerr's smartest moves, as Phoenix's excellent medical staff helped him overcome the injuries that had plagued him for years. Yet it failed to stem the team's decline, and the Suns were eliminated in the first round of the playoffs by—who else?—the Spurs. Once hailed as the team's savior, coach Mike D'Antoni was fired. The next year was even more trying for Kerr. When Stoudemire was sidelined with an eye injury just after the All-Star Game, the team failed to make the postseason for the first time in four years.

The 2009–2010 season saw the Suns recapture some of their old magic. Under coach Alvin Gentry, they led the league in points per game and three-point shooting during the regular season. Relishing being back in the playoffs, Phoenix defeated the Trailblazers in six games and then swept the Spurs. They fought hard against the defending champion Los Angeles Lakers in the Conference Finals, before falling 4–2. Fittingly, the man coaching the Lakers was none other than Phil Jackson. Despite overseeing the team's turnaround, Kerr decided to vacate the general manager role and return to the TNT commentary booth. In 2011, he also began announcing NCAA Tournament matchups on CBS.

Calling games on TV might not seem to have prepared Kerr for what came next, but he later revealed it was very beneficial, particularly because it prepared him to talk with reporters. "The media training is a big help," he said. This wasn't all Kerr learned from his time on TNT and CBS. At the urging of former New York Knicks coach and fellow analyst Jeff Van Gundy, Kerr also created a folder on his computer in which he wrote about various offensive and defensive schemes, compiled scouting reports on players, and made notes about coaches' philosophies, practice schedules, and team policies. By the time he left TNT, Kerr—with help from his friend Kelly Peters, a coach at Torrey Pines High School—had also created a video library with more than fifty plays. He'd soon need every single one of them.[8]

LEADERSHIP REFLECTIONS

- Are you just coasting in your current position, or are you seeking to learn all you can?

- What's a job that you thought was worthless at the time that you can now think back to and find some value in?

- Which colleague could you hit up to help you prepare for the next stage of your leadership journey?

CARROLL'S CORE FOUR

Kerr could have stayed comfortable in his broadcasting role for the rest of his career, but basketball continued calling to him. On May 14, 2014, the Golden State Warriors announced that they had hired him to replace head coach Mark Jackson, who had led the team to fifty-one wins the previous season.

While Kerr had always been a natural leader, he lacked formal experience in such a role. Consequently, his appointment was greeted with widespread skepticism.

USA Today called Kerr's contract "crazy."[9] Bruce Jenkins, a veteran San Francisco sportswriter, wrote that hiring Kerr was "a risky gamble." Deriding Warriors owner Joe Lacob as "pathetic," he issued a doomsday prediction for Kerr's first season in charge. "I don't buy this notion that, with a new coach, these same Warriors reach the NBA Finals next year," wrote Jenkins. "Dead wrong. Zero chance of that."[10]

Determined to prove the doubters wrong, Kerr collated all the information he'd gathered while in broadcasting, consulted with Gregg Popovich and other mentors, and sought advice from master coaches in multiple sports.

One of these was football coach Pete Carroll, who led the University of Southern California Trojans to two national championships and delivered the Seattle Seahawks their first Super Bowl win in 2005. When their conversation turned to building culture, Carroll advised Kerr to come up with ten core values, narrow the list to four, and then get player buy-in. The "Core Four" Kerr came up with were joy, mindfulness, compassion, and competition. Let's look at how he put each one into action from the moment he arrived at his first Warriors training camp in the fall of 2014.

Joy

"As a coach, what I ache for is not just winning the game, but it's that feeling when everybody is connected and joyful and competing together," Kerr told Michael Gervais on the *Finding Mastery* podcast. "There's no feeling like it."[11]

Mindfulness

Kerr's former assistant coach Luke Walton explained the role of mindfulness in the Warriors organization: "It's thinking the game. It's not just trying [to] out-talent people; it's not trying to go for your individual stats. It's being mindful of the right way to do things."[12]

Compassion

"Compassion really encompasses a lot of different things," Kerr said to Positive Coaching Alliance cofounder and CEO Jim Thompson. "Not just on the floor, in a situation . . . where maybe somebody makes a mistake and a teammate goes over and high-fives him or fist-pumps him. Those are really important moments, but [compassion] is every day. The coaching staff having compassion for the players, knowing how hard their jobs are. . . . It's also really important for the team to have compassion for each other, . . . understanding that everybody's got different pressures on them. Acknowledging that in a daily manner really establishes, I think, a good tone for the team, and establishes a good routine, a good environment to work in."[13]

Competition

"Winning has to matter, and to win at this level, you'd better be competitive," Kerr explained to Mackey Craven at Open-View's CEO Forum. "It's important to keep score constantly, to always keep track of who is winning and who is losing, even in practices. But do it in a fun way."[14]

LEADERSHIP REFLECTIONS

- Write down ten values that are important to you as a person and a leader.

- Narrow this list down to your Core Four values.

- How will you reflect these in your daily habits, and what can you do to get your team on board with them?

EVERYONE WANTS TO BE PART OF SOMETHING

Kerr recognized that as important as these values were, they would be useless without the right staff to implement them. So, after giving the matter a lot of thought, he invited his former college teammate Bruce Fraser, defensive stalwart Ron Adams (because, as he knew well from Jackson and Popovich, you need equally potent offense and defense to win titles), NBA champion Luke Walton, former pro Jarron Collins, and veteran coach Alvin Gentry (whom Kerr had also hired in Phoenix) to join him.

It was clear to this brain trust that the Warriors couldn't just embrace Kerr's core values in the locker room; they had to put them into action on the court. That's why they were determined to transform the Warriors from an easy-to-stifle, isolation-heavy team into one that befuddled defenses with selfless passing and player movement. "The more people who are involved in the offense, the more powerful it becomes," Kerr said. Warriors general manager Bob Myers agreed, stating, "All of us want to be part of something."[15]

Sometimes Kerr wasn't seeking consensus, but rather someone to play devil's advocate and contradict him. "Ron is a truth-teller," Kerr told the *Chicago Tribune* after Adams agreed to join him in Oakland. "I wanted somebody who wasn't afraid to say, 'You screwed that up.' We've had our dust-ups in a very productive way."[16]

In addition to selecting a stellar staff committed to pass-first attacking, staunch defending, and values-based coaching, Kerr saw the need to get buy-in from his players. So, he flew out to Miami to meet with small forward Harrison Barnes, got together with "Splash Brothers" Klay Thompson and Steph Curry, and even put his frequent-flyer miles to good use by traveling to Australia to visit veteran center Andrew Bogut.

"That's big, actually making the commitment to fly out and see guys," Barnes told *Sports Illustrated*. "It would've been easy for him to fly and meet Steph and just call everybody else."[17]

Another Kerr tactic to take the Warriors from contenders to champions was bringing in consultants to unlock his team's full potential. One was someone Kerr knew well from his tenure as general manager of the Suns: two-time NBA MVP Steve Nash, who served as a player development consultant for five years, before being named head coach of the Brooklyn Nets. The parallels between Nash and Curry were seemingly endless. Both were undersized guards blessed with ballhandling and shooting skills rather than supernatural athleticism. Both had played at small colleges—Nash at Santa Clara and Curry at Davidson. Both faced chronic injuries: Nash's persistently bad back forced him to lie down when not directing the Suns "seven seconds or less" offense, while Curry's bad ankles put his basketball longevity at stake.

Most crucial, Kerr knew that while Curry could put the ball in the hoop anytime he wanted, for the Warriors to achieve greatness, he had to buy into Kerr's Core Four values as well as Nash's selflessness on and off the court. So, perhaps it's no surprise that, in the 2014–2015 season, Curry won the MVP award, and the following season emulated Nash both in becoming a back-to-back MVP and joining the 50-40-90 club.

LEADERSHIP REFLECTIONS

- Which people from your past could you bring in to bolster your organization?

- Who do you believe could improve your decision-making by challenging your assumptions?

- Which outside consultants could help your team go to the next level?

MASTERING THE MENTAL GAME

The Warriors' long-term success and ability to go from a borderline playoff team to a perennial contender didn't rest on Curry maximizing his talents. He also had to get the most out of Andre Iguodala, Draymond Green, Klay Thompson, and key reserves such as Shaun Livingston, which involved getting them to think like champions. To this end, Kerr followed the example of Phil Jackson, who had brought in George Mumford to lead mindfulness training for the Bulls, and recruited Chris Johnson from the Navy's Operational

Neuroscience Lab in San Diego to serve as a part-time team psychologist.[18] "If you can get somebody who's a better teammate, better character, more coachable, better learner and more calm under stress, and you get a collection of those, you get a better team," Johnson told ESPN.[19]

It soon became clear that Johnson's contribution and Kerr's values-driven, detail-oriented approach had created such a team. In his first season in the Bay, Golden State blasted out of the gate to go 19–2, the best start ever for a rookie coach. By the end of the season, they sat atop the Western Conference with a 67–15 record and, in the playoffs, left the New Orleans Pelicans, Memphis Grizzlies, and Houston Rockets in their wake to win the West. Though LeBron James's Cleveland Cavaliers jumped to a 2–1 lead in the finals, Kerr made a masterful adjustment by starting Iguodala in place of veteran center Andrew Bogut.

The so-called Death Lineup turned the tide and took the series in six games. Kerr had now entered rare company as one of the few to win NBA championships as both a player and coach. And more than simply winning, the team had done it the right way, with an up-tempo, share-first, pass-often style that embodied joy, mindfulness, compassion, and competition. Pete Carroll had urged Kerr to identify these values and then instill them throughout the organization. Fittingly, Iguodala was named Finals MVP, in part due to his willingness to go from a career-long starter to the team's sixth man until the last three games.

· During the Warriors' run to the 1975 NBA title, the team had a banner that read "Togetherness" prominently displayed in their home locker room. Kerr's predecessor, Mark Jackson, had the team cultivate a similar our-team-against-the-world mentality by shouting "Just us" to end time-out huddles, and Kerr granted Curry's request to continue the tradition. They reinforced this with their own locker room sign, which read: "mUSt be jUSt about US." Combined with the four core values Kerr introduced and the whole team bought into, it was team spirit that set these Warriors apart as much as anything they did on the court.[20]

LEADERSHIP REFLECTIONS

- What mental skills—such as confidence, visualization, or gratitude—would you most like to master?

- Which big goals can you target to take your organization from contender to champion?

- How can you adjust your tactics to get more from your personnel?

BRAVING THE BACK ATTACK

Everything seemed to be going perfectly for Kerr and the Warriors. Until it wasn't. After the team won the 2015 championship, the back pain Kerr had been struggling with escalated until he could hardly walk. He decided to have a ruptured disc surgically repaired. As it turned out, his initial pain was just beginning. During the procedure, a dural tear caused spinal fluid to leak, leaving Kerr with excruciating headaches, localized pain, and a host of other symptoms. He had to sit out the first half of the 2015–2016 season, as he rehabbed from secondary surgeries. Though they missed their coach, the Warriors didn't skip a beat on the court.

Kerr's protégé Luke Walton (son of NBA great Bill Walton, who, like Kerr, had played for Lute Olson at Arizona) led the team to an NBA record 24–0 start. This was a testament not only to the team's talent and Kerr's trust in Walton and his assistants, but also to the teamwide buy-in to his core values.

"I actually took a lot of pride in the fact that the team was doing so well while I was out because I recognized that the process had really performed from the previous year, and we were able to carry that over," Kerr said at a gathering of CEOs. This wasn't just about Walton and the rest of the coaching staff, but also the Warriors' players. "It's our job to empower them and get them on the right track so they are equipped to take ownership."[21]

By the time Kerr returned to the Warriors' bench in January 2016, the team was a league-leading 39–4. But his symptoms came on like a tsunami again in April, and Kerr ruled himself out indefinitely, leaving Walton to steer the ship. Nonetheless, the team's "Strength in Numbers" motto proved apt as they closed the regular season like a freight train, finishing 73–9 to break the Bulls' record that many thought would never be bettered.[22] This made Kerr the only person to be a player and coach on 70-win teams. However, a fairy-tale ending was not to be, at least not for this postseason. Although he fought through his ever-worsening pain during the Finals, the Cleveland Cavaliers, led by LeBron James, dug themselves out of a 3–1 hole and defeated the Warriors in seven games to end their chance at a three-peat and conclude James's fairy-tale return to Cleveland.

Kerr and the Warriors had a shot at redemption in the rematch with the Cavaliers the following spring. But try as he might, he couldn't shake the headaches, spasms, and other symptoms that bedeviled him. He handed the head coaching reins to his assistant Mike Brown (who, ironically, coached the Cavs to the 2007 NBA Finals). Like Luke Walton before him, Brown did an admirable job, leading the Warriors to a 12–0 start to the playoffs. Kerr returned to his post in the championship round, in which Steph Curry, Klay Thompson, Draymond Green, and Finals MVP Kevin Durant overwhelmed the Cavs 4–1.

They would repeat this result the following season to lift the Larry O'Brien Championship Trophy for the third time in four years and seal their spot in history as one of the most dominant teams ever. Though Kerr had considered a premature retirement from coaching, he finally got his pain under control and recaptured both his health and the infectious joy that he had instilled in the Warriors from day one. What got him through the toughest time since losing his father? Gratitude. "It's important to go through life counting your blessings," Kerr explained. "Each day being thankful for your family, your career, whatever it is you're thankful for. I think those things need to be acknowledged."[23]

LEADERSHIP REFLECTIONS

- If you had to step aside for a while or permanently, who could you count on to take the reins?

- What are you doing to empower your people to lead?

- What three blessings are you most thankful for today?

WHEN WINNERS LOSE

The loss of his father and his chronic back pain were arguably the greatest struggles in Kerr's life, and he handled each with a mix of grace and determination. But in the 2018–2019 season, he faced a new challenge: losing when he was expected to win. Entering the year with the most successful record of any four-year coach in NBA history, as well as two league MVPs and four All-Stars, everyone from Las Vegas oddsmakers to the media to the Warriors themselves expected the team to rise again to the pinnacle of the game come June.

Though Kerr had overcome his back woes, player health is a fickle thing, even if you have the best medical and training staff around. So it proved, as Kevin Durant went down with a calf strain in Game 5 of a tough Western Conference Finals matchup with the Houston Rockets. The Warriors eventually prevailed to make it back to the Finals for the fifth season in a row. There they faced another Gregg Popovich–shaped player, Kawhi Leonard, the 2014 Finals MVP who had overcome a serious leg injury to lead his new team, the Toronto Raptors, to victory over the Milwaukee Bucks in the Eastern Conference Finals.

On paper, the Warriors should have walloped the Raptors, even with Leonard and mercurial big man Marc Gasol facing them. But with Durant still out and Golden State uncharacteristically shaken, Toronto jumped out to a 3–1 lead. Undaunted, the Warriors bounced back from behind with a combined 57 points from Curry and Thompson. That was the good news. The bad? Despite bravely coming back from his calf strain, Durant sustained an even worse injury, rupturing his Achilles tendon. Convinced they could still stave off elimination, the Warriors came out strong in Game 6, with Thompson pouring in 30 points in 31 minutes. But just as it looked like they might be able to force Game 7, Thompson's knee buckled beneath him as Danny Green challenged his dunk attempt in the third quarter. His game and the shorthanded Warriors' bid for a fourth title was over, as Leonard led the Raptors to their first ever championship and garnered his second Finals MVP trophy.

Everyone expected the team of the decade to regroup, get Thompson and Durant healthy, and make a push back to the basketball summit. Yet while the former quickly inked a new five-year contract (followed by Green, who signed a four-year extension), the latter left, signing with the Brooklyn Nets. More change was on the way, with the Warriors waiving two important members of their three championship teams, Iguodala and Livingston, and the latter promptly retired. Although Kerr and general manager Bob Myers acquired All-Star guard D'Angelo Russell from the Nets as part of the Durant trade, they faced an unprecedented level of instability going into the 2019–2020 season.

Echoing the preternatural calm of his coaching mentors Olson, Jackson, and Popovich, Kerr chose to turn a lot of negatives into a positive, telling *The Athletic:* "Lot of new beginnings—new arena, new roster, and probably some new things, style of play, strategy. We'll figure that out as we go. You always have to see how it looks on the court before you can really establish your identity. I'm excited about the challenge and it's amazing it's only a couple weeks away."[24] Asked what his plan was heading into training camp, Kerr stated: "Re-imagine everything and adapt."[25]

The following season saw Kerr having to live by these words to a greater extent than he had imagined when he spoke them. Golden State not only had to contend with the absence of Thompson as he rehabbed from ACL surgery, they were also without Steph Curry for all but five games when he suffered a broken hand. The team decided that Russell wasn't the right fit, and traded him for talented yet inconsistent Minnesota Timberwolves swingman Andrew Wiggins. Then the NBA shut down in the wake of the COVID-19 pandemic. When it invited eighteen teams to compete in a protocol-protected bubble in Orlando, the Warriors didn't make the cut. In fact, they finished last in the Western Conference and posted the worst record in the NBA at 15–50.

Yet looking ahead to the 2020–2021 NBA season, Kerr was determined that his team would shake off the disappointments of the previous year and the news that they would be without Klay Thompson for a second straight year after the All-Star tore his Achilles tendon. "What's important is really finding the motivation from within, loving the game, loving the preparation and loving the competition," he told the *Mercury News*. "And we have guys who embody that."[26]

LEADERSHIP REFLECTIONS

- What challenge seems like a daunting obstacle right now?

- How can you turn it into an exciting opportunity?

- What can you do to adapt to a new and uncertain situation?

MASTER AND APPRENTICE

To continue developing as a leader, Kerr went back to basics in the offseason. Showing his humility by dismissing the fact that he had had the most successful first five years of any head coach in NBA history, he decided to serve as an assistant to his old mentor Gregg Popovich. Although an undermanned Team USA whose roster featured only one All-Star fell short at the 2019 FIBA World Cup in China, Kerr used the opportunity to learn some more important lessons from the man with more than 1,200 wins to his credit.

"It's more detail stuff in terms of how he operates in practice and how he handles the team," Kerr said. "It's not really about plays and drills. It's more about efficiency and process."[27]

Part of the benefit to Kerr was observing Popovich from a different angle. Rather than facing the man who has won five championships and three NBA Coach of the Year awards as he did during the twilight of his playing career, the student was now standing alongside his master. "I'm getting to watch Pop up close for the first time," Kerr said. "I played for him but I've never coached with him. The experience has been fantastic."[28]

During the COVID-19 pandemic, during which his Warriors didn't make it into the NBA bubble at Disney World in Orlando due to the absence of Klay Thompson, Steph Curry's broken hand, and the departure of Kevin Durant and other key veterans, Kerr also seized the opportunity to collaborate with another mentor who set him on the path of excellence as a coach: Pete Carroll. The two championship-winning leaders teamed up for the *Flying Coach* podcast to discuss themes as diverse as analytics, politics, and draft strategy.

More than just two good ol' boys talking shop, the podcast also gave listeners the chance to hear from guests such as Brené Brown, Bill Murray, and Michael Lewis, all while raising money for COVID-19 relief charities.

When Kerr first reached out to Carroll soon after taking the Warriors head coaching job, it might have seemed to outsiders that it was a one-way exchange: the proven veteran football coach advising the basketball sideline newbie. But in the first episode of *Flying Coach*, Carroll revealed that he found just as much value in Kerr's visit to the Seattle Seahawks facility and that mentoring is always a two-way exchange. "I took it as an opportunity to dig in and rethink how I would advise someone," Carroll said. "It helped me understand more clearly what's important to me."[29]

Kerr revealed that his trip to CenturyLink Field (known as Lumen Field since November 2020) in Seattle began when his friend and former Jets general manager Mike Tannenbaum asked which coaches Kerr admired in other sports. The Seahawks had just won their first Super Bowl, but beyond their on-field success, Kerr was captivated by how Carroll got his team to play with such joy and enthusiasm. Upon hearing this, Tannenbaum reached out to Seahawks defensive coordinator Dan Quinn and set up Kerr's trip to Seattle.

One of the things that struck Kerr from the get-go was that Carroll didn't want him to be a passive bystander at practice, but to get in the thick of things with the players and coaching staff. "During a scrimmage I was standing off to the side, and you said, 'Go get in the huddle. Listen to Russell [Wilson] call the play,'" Kerr told Carroll on the *Flying Coach*.[30] Arguably the most important teaching moment came on the third day of Kerr's visit, when Carroll ushered him into his office for a talk about what Kerr planned to do differently with the Warriors, a playoff-caliber team that was yet to fulfill its full potential.

Initially, Kerr thought that Carroll was asking him about the specifics of his offense, which had taken him two years to design. But that wasn't what Carroll was getting at. To make his point, he told Kerr how he learned to become a coach while apprenticing as an assistant to San Francisco 49ers legend Bill Walsh.

"What came through wasn't any of the particulars, but how he was really adamant and emphatic about the things that were important to him, and execution, discipline, and practice," Carroll said. "With Coach Walsh, it was all about knowing who you are. So, that's why I wanted to get you to start thinking about who are you as a coach. What are you all about? Where are you coming from? What's important to you? What are your uncompromising principles? What do you stand for? Because you're going to be in camp and some guy's not going to show up at a meeting, he's going to be late for the team bus, and then he's going to spout off at one of your players in a game. Every time you deal with any situation, you're making a statement about who you are. It's got nothing to do with X's and O's. [The players] are going to watch you and see if you believe in something or if you're just dealing with things randomly."[31]

"Everything you're talking about ends with authenticity, right?" Kerr replied. "Everyone talks about culture. We've all been in a gym where there's a big sign that says, 'Only the strong survive' and you're like, 'What does that even mean?' What I learned from you was everything that happens in prac-tice, everything that the players feel when they walk into the gym or onto the field, every day that they come to the facility, it has to be real. And the values that are important to you as a coach have to come alive. That's how culture is defined. And when your players feel that, they feel that authenticity coming from you and it comes alive in practice, now there's something real and the momentum starts to build."[32]

That momentum, the core values he came up with at Carroll's urging, and the realization that "what coaching is all about is serving your players" propelled Kerr to the best coaching start in NBA history and a 2016 NBA Coach of the Year Award.[33] It also spurred the Warriors to three championships and breaking the Chicago Bulls' single season win tally with an astonishing 73–9 record.

LEADERSHIP REFLECTIONS

- Whom have you served under in the past and could still learn more from?

- What's an opportunity in your profession or a volunteer role where you could take a lesser position and get a different perspective?

- Having achieved success, are you stuck in a fixed mindset? If so, how can you switch to a growth mindset and continue rounding out your skill set?

SUMMARY

This chapter told an unconventional story: Undersized guard with minimal athleticism makes it to the NBA, wins five titles, and finishes his career as the all-time leading three-point shooter. General manager and head coach with no experience turns one team around and leads another to NBA immortality. Perennial winner faces losing and a career-ending back injury and overcomes both. Every stage of Steve Kerr's journey as a player, coach, and leader could be viewed as unlikely. Yet with each step, he soaked up his mentors' knowledge like a sponge, viewed adverse situations as learning opportunities, and squeezed every ounce of potential out of himself. In the following chapters, we'll use his example as a launching point to explore themes such as the importance of self-care, mission-driven focus, and other traits that define the Leader's Mind.

CHAPTER 3

GRACE UNDER PRESSURE

I had a moment where I was not sure it was going to end in a landing. And at that moment, I had the thought that it would be the day I'm meeting Jesus face to face. But instead of dwelling on that horrific thought that this could be the end, I said to myself: "You know what? I won't be a stranger. This is the Lord that I strive to meet with every day."

—TAMMIE JO SHULTS, *Southwest Pilot of Flight 1380*

Flight 1380 was a regularly scheduled passenger flight from New York's LaGuardia Airport to Dallas Love Field. Tammie Jo Shults, a former United States Navy pilot, was the captain of the flight, and Darren Ellisor, a former United States Air Force pilot, was the first officer. There were 144 passengers and five crew members on board.

As the flight captain, Shults took control of the plane after an uncontained engine failure caused debris to damage the fuselage, depressurizing the cabin. Tragically, one passenger died. How many leaders experience such a moment, when the fates of dozens are in their hands? How would most react? What does one draw upon to do what must be done?

There are three key formative arcs that gave this captain nerves of steel. The first was upbringing: Tammie Jo Shults had a lifetime of challenges and opportunities to learn how to respond to a situation. Second, mentors are vital: they build up your capacity, influence your leadership approach, and ultimately provide insight into how to lead a team.

Third, dealing with a situation: when to engage, when to take a break.

RESPONSIBILITY AND OWNERSHIP

There is little in the background of Shults's childhood that indicates a future-pilot-in-the-making. She grew up on a farm with parents who had nothing to do with aviation. As Shults herself mentions, economics and a young dream were the main factors:

> Truthfully, economics is part of what drove the direction of flying for me into the military, because I really didn't know any pilots, my family wasn't involved in anything aviation, and on a farm or ranch, cash is the least of what we produce. I'd always admired our military and what they stood for and what they stand in between us and the world for. But, yeah, I would have to say it was [a case of] making flying a realistic plan, not just day-dreaming: "Okay, how do you get this into a workable plan?" And, economically, the military was it.

Although Shults is very matter-of-fact about her initial aspirations, it is clear from talking with her that this characteristic also developed over time in how she was raised.

> I think a big part of my experience of lessons in leadership that I look back at and notice in my parents would not boil down to words. They would give you a responsibility and the authority that goes with that to get it done. If we were told to work the field and some

piece of equipment that we normally would use—a tractor, trailer, whatever—wasn't working, my parents didn't want us to come back and ask, "Okay, what should we do because the tractor won't start?"

We had the authority to go get whatever we needed to get it done. And I just remember that kind of situation sometimes, just how much [responsibility] we kids had when we were ten and twelve years old. I think that part is allowing the people that work with you and for you to take ownership in it. Not just to feel like servants that are appointed a task to do, but to own it, too.

This sense of ownership and getting things done is vital to successful leadership. Later on in her life, these same patterns, habits, and attitudes were conveyed to Shults's crew and flight staff.

My focus was flying the airplane. I've been asked a number of times if I was worried about the people in the back. And my answer is that I knew they were being taken care of as well as they could be. Because I'd already seen how the [flight attendants] reacted to people in the calmness of boarding and being more than just a person standing in their position for boarding. They welcomed people; they had the energy to assist. They were outgoing in their welcome. And therefore, I knew they weren't the type to ignore people when they were in need. And so I could take it off my mental checklist. I didn't have the weight of worrying about those in the back because, quite frankly, there was nothing I could do for them. I knew they had a good crew to attend to them, and so I focused on flying the aircraft.

THE MEANING OF MENTORSHIP

Having role models is key to the trajectory of any leader. While many concentrate on the individual qualities of a leader, how often do we actually hear the leaders themselves say that it was mostly luck, or the good fortune to bump into someone, or owing it all to a few decisive moments where a trusted mentor nudged things along? Let's take a look at Shults's mentors and then at how she describes herself as the mentor in her own commercial flight crew:

> One of the things I remember my dad talking about was that he was the youngest of eight by a long way and tended to get picked on at school. Even though he grew to be six foot two, he was a small kid. I remember him telling us that he had his lunch always getting raided by the bigger kids. So, he got some sheep pellets one day, covered them with chocolate, and put them in his lunch bag. That was the last time his lunch got raided.

Obviously, Shults's father learned to take care of things. His approach wasn't always just an instinctive, instantaneous, direct retaliatory punch to the bully's face. In fact, the approach that one takes is often as important as the final result.

Later, as a groundbreaking female pilot, Shults was not spared from the vestiges of the military's old boy network that included discrimination and disrespect from peers and superiors. How she dealt with this situation reflects on what made her a great leader. To gain this maturity, however, she had some good mentors. Shults recounts an important mentor in the military, Rosemary Mariner, an American pilot and one of the first six women to earn their wings as United States naval aviators in 1974. She was the first female military pilot to fly a tactical jet, and the first to achieve command of an operational aviation squadron.[1] In Shults's own words:

Rosemary was definitely a huge mentor in my life. Just knowing her as a junior officer coming into her squadron, I was impressed with how she was not reactionary to what other people said or did, and she definitely listened. She took in all of the information, but she would calmly think about and decide what was the action to be taken.

There were a number of things that she could have been very upset by and she just refused to be offended, because that would cloud her judgment. Offenses grow the more you think about them so they can really obscure your vision of the facts. That's the human element we have to deal with. I loved to see her in action. For instance, she had done a lot of work making sure [my husband] Dean and I would get detailed to the same coast.

And then the eighty-seventh commanding officer said he was sending Dean to the other coast, which is where everybody but Dean wanted to go. It was very pointed and intended either to split us up, or get me out early, or send me to the other coast following him.

I'm not sure, other than just being ugly, what his purposes were. I can only guess at those.

When I told Rosemary, I liked how she responded. I did not want to spend the next two years on the opposite coast from my husband, and so I said, "I'm planning to put in for a transfer."

And she replied, "Well, let's wait on that and see what we can do." The captain who was sending Dean to the other coast outranked her by a long shot. She was a commander, not a captain, but she just quietly went about making the phone calls that would make a difference and got it all changed back to what it had been. And she never commented on it. She never told anyone about her victory and overcoming that.

She saw how the black sailors dealt with the sideways attacks and took a note from it. A lot of it was dealt with humor. And she said they also made sure that they had a certain camaraderie such that they didn't just sequester themselves. So, when somebody offended me, it wasn't, "I'm not having anything to do with them." This was a strategy of staying in the ballgame.

You don't have to be a part of the inner group to still be in the ballgame. In fact, she constantly read and tried to stay in the game. I can say I also tried to. She was a brilliant woman. She stayed abreast of what was going on, not just in her squadron, but what was coming ahead in the future of the Navy.

Rosemary Mariner died on January 24, 2019, following a five-year battle with ovarian cancer. Her final assignment

was as the Chairman of the Joint Chiefs of Staff's Professor
of Military Studies at the National War College.[2]

From this important mentor, Shults learned to "stay in
the game" for a successful military career. Her mentor gave
her insight into how to navigate the field as well as how to
deflect and deal with criticism.

Later on, as a pilot and captain at Southwest Airlines,
Shults provided leadership in both word and deed. Along
with flying the plane and taking control in a critical situation, she regularly did small things to increase interaction
with her flight attendants to gain an evaluation of passengers
coming on board. In addition, she empowered others on her
team so that she could concentrate on flying the plane. Such
teamwork was part of the reason she was able to bring down
a crippled aircraft safely. Here is how she describes it:

> The captain sets the tone. If the captain wants to just
> head to the cockpit, do what they do, and not take part
> in anything, then everybody more or less feels like
> they're on their own. To create teamwork, the captain
> is in charge of making sure everybody has what they
> need. Flying comes after you push off the gate. Off gate,
> you should be the on-site point of contact. There are
> different things that can go smoothly if the captain is
> available to make decisions that need to be made. How-
> ever, if that question is held in balance, and it just takes
> time, you wind up not getting done what you need to.
>
> If the flight attendants know that they have your
> attention, not just if there's a catastrophic medical emer-
> gency, but even when they just have a question about
> somebody or something, that's vital. We always meet

with the new crew to do a captain's briefing, which includes the weather, where you're going, and different things to do with the flights that day. But if at all possible, I try to bring coffee for the crew, or maybe iced tea in the afternoon, or chocolates or something so that everybody hangs around a while longer, and we chitchat a little bit.

I include in my brief that if they see something that sets off their flying radar, that they let me know. They have a good sense of what the flying public should look and act like. And if something strikes them as odd, let us know and we'll address it on the ground before we get going.

Here's an example. There happened to be a young lady that had had an allergic reaction that required her to have an EpiPen with her. They never figured out why she'd had this allergic reaction, and she's a grown woman traveling by herself. But she got a little nervous and asked the flight attendant if she could just keep an eye on her in case she had an allergic reaction. The attendant was fairly new and young, so she wasn't really sure how to address it.

And so she asked to come back to weigh in on the situation. We found a very easy fix to it all. If there is some kind of dialogue, rather than just a monologue laid down at the beginning of the brief, then little questions that crop up don't need to culminate in somebody being taken off the flight very often. This happens at the beginning when you meet. Captains have a responsibility on the ground that's just as heavy as when they get airborne.

Shults mentions that she felt it was her role as captain to take over the controls from the copilot on that fateful flight, but she needed to rely on her crew to do this.

Well, that's procedure for, I think, any airline—definitely procedure at Southwest—that captains land emergency situations. That's usually practical due to two things. The captain usually has more time in than the first officer. They definitely have more time at Southwest and that is why they're sitting on the captain side. They're the ones who sign for the aircraft and are ultimately responsible at the end of the day. That is something that's a little more of a mechanical decision rather than my personal decision. Now, *when* you take it, that is a personal decision.

On our flight that day, I knew we were definitely having a pretty steep descent, and I needed to have time to fly the aircraft myself to feel the controllability of it before we got close to the ground. I was in a position to do that a little earlier than ten thousand feet. Being at the center of the controls and the fact that we had an aircraft that was a bit of a handful, it was tough to communicate. That was another big part of it—communicating—which was still a little cumbersome even after we got our masks on. Having divided it up earlier with me flying and communicating with Air Traffic Control and [First Officer] Darren taking on all the other systems and communication with the back kept us from having the cumbersome situation of one person flying, one person talking to ATC. It's a double check on a good day, but on a bad day, it streamlines it a little bit more to do it the way that we did it, where we divided and conquered.

[Communicating] is a huge part of leadership. First of all, having names for the people that you're working with, not just the flight attendants, but also the first officer: Darren, Shanique, Catherine, and Rachel. Having some personal interaction with the people that you work with, because you don't trust people you don't know.

So, again, creating an atmosphere where there's a little bit of a dialogue so that you're sure you're going to be hearing from those people if they need something or see something. Because as the leader, as the captain, you're not going to know everything that's going on. You need their information. They're going to see more than you will.

[In Jesus] we had such a great example of servant leadership, and in Matthew, Mark, Luke, and John. And I realized Christians see that, read that, know about that, but it's not automatic to pull it into your leadership style. It takes stitching it together. You know we see it in Christ, we admire it, but does it really change with how we treat people, how we go about leading people? And this is another thing that I think is so pivotal—he never pushed people into doing things. He pulled them into it. And I think that's a huge part of being a good leader, whether it's a dad at home, mom leading the kids, or a captain at an airline. People are inspired to do things rather than instructed.

There are some important leadership questions to ask from Shults's compelling account. Do you enable and communicate with your team? Can you rely on them when you need to make an important decision? Do you know their names? Whom do you trust?

ENGAGING AND DISENGAGING

Leaders often want to do everything; they are always on the go. But sometimes it's necessary to take a break, step back, and realize that absorbing and evaluating the situation requires time. According to Shults:

> I guess part of that goes back to when I was younger and would get really anxious about something going on at school, like a test. My parents pulled the plug on that and said: "Oh, I'm sorry, you're going to need to go get your jeans on. We need you to help us out" with whatever project, whether it was vaccinating hogs or swabbing or picking up hay bales.
>
> They would see that anxiety building up, and they would redirect my energy. And honestly that was such a great lesson for me that I've used my whole life. If something just doesn't seem to have an answer to it or you can't progress there, get your mind and your body on something else. It doesn't make the problem go away, but sometimes distance can give you perspective.
>
> I kind of have a laundry list. My routine in the morning is that the first person that I like to write on my mental compass of the day is the Lord and his

work. Putting my day before the Lord helps. Working out is also a great way to clear my mind and some nervous energy. Then maybe going flying in our family plane. I don't golf well, please know that, but I go to be outside and hit a golf ball.

During some of the busiest times, I would have to stop, put it all down, and go coach javelin for an hour or two. I had kids from seven years old to seventeen, and it was a good break. I'd go coach javelin, laugh at some of their high school jokes, and, like I said, get a little different perspective. Sometimes we get our heads so far into a problem that we really can't see the forest through the trees.

[During the flight with the engine failure] I just stepped away from that realizing: "Okay, so that's the worst of the bad news. The good news is we're still flying." Truthfully, for all pilots, a big part of piloting is compartmentalization. Because there are enough moving parts on a good day to which you need to pay attention. And so compartmentalizing and forgetting about your kids' grades, their friends, their volleyball game, their football game, your leaking roof, or whatever is going on at home, it has to be set aside to fly. That's on a good day. Just that practice of compartmentalization is huge. And then, yes, experience and training.

I would say experience weighs in just as heavily as training. And then to give the Lord the credit. Truthfully, having a calmness that I don't think I have naturally, that was a gift. I don't think that that was all just due to my training and my experience. But definitely a gift in being able to not just focus on what we were doing, but to be creative on the way down.

Because we had to change our plans a number of times, when we realized that we didn't have the thrust available we thought we could use, which means we would have to recalculate getting from where we were to the runway, as more or less a glider. And with just a certain amount of thrust available.

And at that moment, I will say I did have that thought that it would be the day I'm meeting Jesus face-to-face. But instead of focusing on that horrific thought that this could be the end, I said to myself: "You know what? I won't be a stranger. This is the Lord that I strive to meet with every day."

While compartmentalizing is an important aspect of leadership, it is also important to engage in ways that may allow you to see through silos. For example, Shults often took a few extra moments to help out her crew, which allowed her to gain a better assessment of the day. Notably, such interaction and observation often allowed her to head off problems on the ground that might have impacted the flight while it was in the air.

At Southwest, I think there's a number of pilots that will go back there [to the passenger area of a plane]. It's usually the captain . . . Well, I say, excuse me, that's not always true. The first officers at Southwest have so much to do sitting in their seats working through inputting weather and a flight plan and things like that into the computer. As a captain, a walkthrough has a threefold purpose really. I see the flight attendants and tell them, "I need the workout; I sit still the whole time." Going through, bending over, picking up trash, and crossing seat belts across the seats is good for me.

Also [if I don't do this], I don't really see my flight attendants, just the one up front throughout the day, unless I work my way back through the cabin. And the only time to do that is really when you're picking up trash and crossing seat belts. It also lets me see what they're dealing with. For example, on some flights, it only took me a few moments in the cabin to go back there after a young sports team or even an older team had been on board, and see how it looked like they had a food fight and thrown everything possible on the floor. It was just horrendous.

It gave me a little clue. And so whenever there is a team or a group of any kind that comes on board, I'll find out who their sponsor is and I'll tell them: "I'd really like to know where you're from so I can write your school and tell your principal how well you represent them." And so, even though I put it in a way that they think, *Oh, that'd be great*, I also have that address to write and let the principal know: "You know what? Your team was a disgrace to your school in the way they behaved on this airplane."

Also, if there are crew members who have decided picking up trash is beneath them and they'd rather be checking their phone for social media updates, that comes to a halt when they see the captain coming back, picking up trash that they should be picking up. There are just so many facets of getting in there and being a part of it. It really is just to help the people that have been serving that whole time and to get to see if there's anything going on.

Sometimes they've heard some rattle in the back or they're having a little trouble with their coffeepot or something that they wouldn't typically call up front for. But if they see me face-to-face, I get to hear about it. Then I take care of it. It solves a lot of problems earlier.

There are various approaches to leadership. What is your leadership style? What approaches would you take in a particular situation? Does the approach address your true goals? In Shults's role as a captain of a flight carrying dozens of people, there is more than just the aircraft's mechanical safety to consider; there are also human elements to deal with, both from the passenger side and also with the crew. Shults describes it like this:

I think sometimes the best leaders are groomed by the people who don't push for the front. They take the time to listen and look and see what the people in the back or on the sideline are dealing with. So, when you are a leader, you know what the real issues are. Not just what's right here in front of me and my job description.

If you know what everybody else is dealing with [it informs what you do]. Dean and I both have commuted for twenty-five years to wherever we start a flight, and we talk to the flight attendants in the back.

In doing that, we get to see a lot of what goes on in the cabin. And I can't help but think that has helped us both be better captains. For example, whenever it's rough and rolling around and the captain makes an announcement, the captain will ask the flight attendants to be seated. Often I've seen somebody reach out and ring their flight attendant call button, and it's still just crazy rocking and rolling. They are required by law to get up and go see, because it could be a medical emergency that needs to be addressed. And then that person will hand them trash.

And I'm thinking, you're kidding me. They are sacrificing. I mean we've had flight attendants bouncing off the ceiling, hurt, with a broken leg, broken ankle, or broken arm from turbulence from not being seated and buckled up. So, one of the things that I've always added to my announcement is, "It's rough. We've asked our flight attendants to be seated, and the flight attendant call button is now emergency only, until it's safe for them to be up." And this comes as an added reminder to people that they don't have suction cups on their feet either, so just hold on, we'll find the smoother air. But unless you're back there, I don't know that you would think about it. Sometimes it's important to go to the back and see a little bit more than just what your job description outlines.

What advice would Shults give to an up-and-coming leader who is confronting adversity? Where does one look for inspiration? What tactics keep one going? Challenges may appear, such as the gender discrimination Shults experienced, or it could be a family crisis thousands of miles away that one is unable to do anything about. How does a person focus on leading oneself and those around him or her? What if a young leader is facing a challenge that seems insurmountable? From a practical standpoint, even if one lacks the experience that others have, what tactic or mantra could they employ to keep pushing through the adversity? Shults reflects on a larger purpose, a greater spirit:

> Well, I can only tell you what I use myself. And it's not a tagline so I can't put it into something snappy. But I absolutely tell the Lord about the problem. I mean I approach it first on my knees because we all tend to take care of what we can take care of ourselves. I think God takes joy in seeing how we solve problems. That's part of being created in his image—having some initiative and being creative. But there does get to be an end to what we can take care of ourselves.

> Especially when it's coming from the outside, it's not up to us to decide how this is going to be taken care of or done and it's out of our hands. Then it's into hands that are, quite frankly, not worthy hands to be making decisions. But that's where the decision is and it's unfair and often malevolent.

> But when we tell the Lord about it, we do two things. First of all, we're telling somebody for whom we don't even have to fill in all the details. He knows the details, but we're also letting him know that, "It's up to you, Lord. I've done my best and I am here asking for your direction." And sometimes his direction is to be quiet and to be patient. And sometimes his

guidance is to get going in a different direction. Maybe it's the same direction, more energy.

I can't tell you how many times I really fell back from the blow of what happened, but I wasn't finished, because God is so much more than what our current circumstances are. It was just reliance on the Lord, and I didn't come upon that on my own. I mean, having read through Old Testament stories much of my life, and then going into the New Testament as well, you can see person after person: Daniel, Joseph, Moses, Ruth, Esther . . . you see these characters that are good, they've done their best, and people have done horrible things to them, but they don't forget God, and God never forgets them.

And sometimes I think we will get to see earthly victories, and sometimes we won't, but that's not the endgame.

SUMMARY

This chapter presented excerpts from an interview with a pioneering navy pilot, Tammie Jo Shults. Later, as flight captain for Southwest Flight 1380, she maintained a calm composure and safely brought a crippled plane back to the ground after a catastrophic engine failure. Through her accounts of being raised on a farm, the mentorship that she received while in the military, and her approach to leading her flight crew, we gain insight into how leaders develop.

She talks about survival in the military, and how she learned to "stay in the game" against ingrained attitudes.

We see how her attitude and approach to problems were nurtured on a farm, where kids as young as ten years old were expected to sort out tractor breakdowns. Most important, a strong, lifelong, spiritual belief gave her perspective and comfort in many of her most challenging moments.

CHAPTER 4

THE MAN IN BLACK

Keep trying to do everything a little bit better—that's the key to continual improvement and success. Do your best, don't be a dickhead, and be a good person.

—NIC GILL, *New Zealand All Blacks'*
Strength and Conditioning Coach

Think back to your first day at a job that you were really excited about. I bet you wanted everything to go as smoothly as possible, from a traffic-jam-less commute to the office to pleasant conversations with your colleagues to, if you were really lucky, doing something that impressed your boss. It is unlikely that your wife having your first child fits in with this imaginary, picture-perfect day one. Yet that's exactly the scenario Nic Gill found himself in upon his debut working with a rugby team in a remote New Zealand region. He was stressed nearly out of his mind.

The ensuing twenty years took Gilly, as everyone fortunate enough to be a friend refers to him, to the pinnacle of the sporting world. Today, he knows that first day foreshadowed the need to work hard to balance family and vocation.

For most of those two decades, Gill has served as head strength and conditioning coach for the most celebrated team in rugby. The New Zealand All Blacks—so called for their trademark monochrome uniforms—aren't merely titans of the rugby pitch, but also the winningest team in sports history, having won a whopping 77 percent of their games in 110 years. Certainly, the '92 Dream Team, Manchester United's famed treble-winning side, and the New England Patriots secured their places in the team sports pantheon, but none can top the consistent excellence of the All Blacks, which extends all the way back to 1903.

WOULD I GO TO WAR WITH YOU?

Few people in world rugby command as much respect as Steve Hansen. Though the All Blacks would ultimately lose to England in his final Rugby World Cup match in 2019, Hansen's record is nothing short of remarkable. He cut his coaching teeth under the watchful eyes of his legendary countrymen Robbie Deans and Wayne Smith at Canterbury Crusaders. He then endured the toughest spell of his career as head coach of the Welsh national team, losing eleven successive test matches before righting the ship with a courageous performance in the 2003 Rugby World Cup.

The following year, Graham Henry, then the All Blacks' head coach, brought Hansen back to his native New Zealand as assistant coach. The two were a formidable partnership that culminated in the All Blacks winning the 2011 Rugby World Cup (which you'll read more about later in this chapter). Later that season, Henry stepped down and Hansen, his heir apparent, was promoted to the head coaching role. In 2013, after leading New Zealand to a decisive 3–0 record in their tour of Ireland and a tenth successive Bledisloe Cup victory over Australia, Hansen was named World Rugby Coach of the Year.

That year, they soared to even greater heights, finishing the season undefeated. With a legendary crop of talent that included not only skipper Richie McCaw but also the sport's leading points scorer Dan Carter, future two-time World Player of the Year Beauden Barrett, and breakthrough star Nehe Milner-Scudder, Hansen's men marched all the way to a second straight Rugby World Cup victory as they trounced Australia 34–17. In 2018, Hansen's All Blacks won the sixth Rugby Championship title of his reign, and claimed the bronze medal in his final game by beating Wales in the Rugby World Cup the following summer.

You might assume that such a coach, who amassed an amazing 93 victories in 107 Test matches (an 87 percent win rate) would be a top-down manager who controlled every aspect of his staff's and squad's existence. But Gill revealed that the truth is very different. While he was dedicated to "leading ordinary blokes to do extraordinary things," as Hansen put it in a 2018 documentary, Hansen was a collaborative leader who sought the advice of his colleagues, mentors, and players.[1] Here is how Nic Gill describes the team's standard of leadership:

> At the All Blacks, leadership is very much a shared model of operation. As a leader, Steve Hansen made the final call, but he liked pulling in his people to share their expertise, so he wasn't in isolation when making tough decisions.
>
> I like to be inspired, so a leader has to be inspiring. They need to create a feeling among the people they're leading that they have everything they need to

be empowered and do what's expected of them. It ultimately comes down to this: Would I go to battle with
you? Would I put my life on the line for you? With
Graham Henry, Steve Hansen, and now Ian Foster, my
answer is, "Yes."

Steve always led by example. The old saying of
"You can't lead others if you can't lead yourself" is
something we always throw at our athletes. First and
foremost, you've got to be able to lead yourself to do
all the right things at the right time, under pressure
and fatigue. Only then will others be willing to follow
you. With Steve, I knew he had my back, that I could
trust him, and that he was always going to do what
was best for the whole group. So, I was willing to follow his lead.

A leader has to display all those attributes they
want to see in others and be willing to walk the walk.
It's easy to say things, but words are meaningless if
they're not lived. Whatever a leader says, they must
also do. It's the same on the field. The players must
be able to look left and right and see that the men
standing alongside them can be counted on to put
their bodies on the line when things get tough. Not
just once but for the full eighty minutes. It's a war out
there and you must be able to rely on your teammates
to do everything that's required of them in every
game and practice, week in and week out.

LEADERSHIP REFLECTIONS

- In what situation could you include your team to make a better decision?

- How are you empowering your people to make their best possible contribution?

- Would people say that you're "walking the walk" of a principled leader?

PROGRESSING FROM PRESCRIPTIVE TO INCLUSIVE LEADERSHIP

Think of a famous leader, and you can probably conjure a characteristic trait that defines that person's leadership style. Maybe it's Bobby Knight's fiery intensity, Margaret Thatcher's iron will, or Marcus Aurelius's unflappable calm. Yet it's a mistake to think that such leaders were always this way. Commonly, events that unfold over the course of years shape a leader's character, personality, and modus operandi. Consequently, that leader learns how to lead more effectively and progress in communicating to and guiding others, as Gill describes:

> I'm a big collaborator and like working with people, so my leadership style reflects that. When I started coaching, my attitude was more like, "You have to do this because it will make you better." I used to be a prescriptive coach. But experience has taught me that

unless the people you're leading are paddling in the same direction as you, you won't get any traction.

I've learned that collaboration is the best way for me to achieve success for the people I work with. I've got ideas, methods, and ways that I want things done, but I don't discount what the person and athlete feels and experiences. I have to engage the athlete and leverage off how they're feeling and what they're thinking. This is a crucial part of taking people where you want them to go.

LEADERSHIP REFLECTIONS

- How has your leadership style progressed over time?

- Where are you on the continuum between prescriptive and inclusive leadership?

- How do you want to continue to evolve your leadership to take the needs of others into account?

HITTING THE COMEBACK TRAIL

For a team as used to winning as the All Blacks, every single loss comes as a shock and draws the ire of New Zealand's fanatical supporters and media. Defeat carries an even greater weight when it comes at the most prestigious competition in the sport: the Rugby World Cup. Heading into the 2019 contest for the Webb Ellis Cup, the All Blacks were once again the favorites to retain their title and achieve the first-ever three-peat. Yet when they encountered the Eddie Jones–led England team in the midst of a transcendent run of form, the All Blacks fell to a startling 19–7 defeat in the semifinal. Although the entire organization took the defeat hard at the time, Gill said, they came out determined to learn from it and return to their winning ways wiser and more resilient than ever.

> For many of our players and staff, it was the first time they'd lost a Rugby World Cup game, so it stung. We're sorry and there was no excuse. We just got [beaten] by the better team on the day. But we refused to sweep the defeat under the rug. The question I'm asking myself and the players is, "How does this fuel you for every practice, every gym session, every day you get up before the next World Cup?"
>
> After we lost in the quarterfinal in 2007, we took a long, hard look at ourselves and figured out what we needed to fix. It's the same this time. Everyone could have scattered after the tournament, but the team stuck together, got off the plane as a unit, and faced the media when we got home. It's something none of us ever want to feel again. When you fail at your first crack, you're bound to be fired up the second time. Half of that team is young enough that they should still be with us at the next World Cup, and they're going to be stronger and more competitive.

LEADERSHIP REFLECTIONS

- How do you rally your team after a defeat?

- What can you do to reframe a recent setback as a new opportunity?

- The next time your group loses, how can you honestly and proactively assess what went wrong so you do better the next time?

WANTING TO BE THE BEST IN THE WORLD

For the All Blacks, winning alone is never good enough. It's competing in the right way and representing the famed black jersey well that count. Tactics must change for each opponent, and not every game can end with a five or six try winning margin. The All Blacks hold themselves to a higher standard than most teams: Domination and excellence aren't optional, but required.

Aspiring to and sustaining such a high level of performance is never easy and comes at a cost. It involves putting in total effort consistently, both individually and on a team level. Everyone knows that when they step onto the field to perform the intimidating *haka* (a traditional Maori dance/challenge), the All Blacks follow by hurling more than 115 years of hard-won pride and passion at their opponents. According to Gill, this warrior spirit is just as all-encompassing for the coaching staff.

> You might recognize that you're really good at what you do, but then you have to acknowledge that you're

definitely not the very best. Yet you want to be, so you get up every day, put in the effort, and keep chasing that elusive dream of one day being the best person in the world at your job. That's not for you to judge, and even if someone was to perceive it, it's still never something you can truly attain.

Some people look at a mantra like "Sweep the sheds" and think that's the secret of the All Blacks' success. But there is no recipe. We've moved on to other things. Culture can't be created overnight by doing or saying this or that, otherwise there would be a lot more organizations with a record of sustained excellence. It is a living and breathing thing, and it needs to be constantly fed by the people within it. You need to be careful because it takes a long time to build up a winning culture, and it can break down very easily. We're lucky to have a group of amazing players and staff. They're the ones that drive the culture every day.

Nobody on our management team or in our playing group ever thinks they've made it. If you start to believe that, you're in a lot of trouble. We always try to be quietly confident but also humble. All you can do is go about your business and give your all in your role for the benefit of the people around you and the family you have to leave behind when you're living out of a suitcase for several months a year. Keep trying to do everything a little bit better—that's the key to continual improvement and success. Do your best, don't be a dickhead, and be a good person.

LEADERSHIP REFLECTIONS

· As a leader, how are you pushing yourself to be the best in the world every day?

· How can you allow your people to shape your culture?

· What are three areas of potential improvement and growth for you personally and your team?

TAKING LIFE LESSONS FROM THE BEST RUGBY PLAYER EVER

Richie McCaw is the only national team captain to guide the country's team to two Rugby World Cup wins (in 2011 and 2015). He also captained the All Blacks to ten Bledisloe Cup wins, four Tri Nations titles, and three Rugby Championship victories. Though rarely the biggest, fastest, or strongest player among the All Blacks' group of athletic All-Stars, his diverse skill set, sheer force of will, and ability to rally his teammates in every situation set McCaw apart. Since Gill's earliest days on the team, he said, its legendary captain made an indelible mark through his fearless leadership by example:

> I vividly remember a team meeting at an airport hotel in Auckland before we flew to play the Springboks in South Africa in 2008. It was five thirty in the morning and our flight was at 8:00 a.m. The manager was telling us about the travel plan, where we were going, where we were staying, and all the logistics.

Richie stood up and said, "All the staff, get out." And I was thinking, *What's going on?* because I was new to the group. I sat outside the meeting room and all the staff were there yapping away. They obviously knew what was going on. It turned out that Richie was telling the team what he expected from them this week. He was basically firing the troops up before we got on the plane.

Two days later, I was walking down a big hallway and Richie was coming the other way. He looked like he was going into battle. His face was blank, he was utterly focused, and there was no small talk. This was five days before the game. It was very much Richie. He was so driven to win that everything he did or thought was about the game and winning on Saturday. Nothing else mattered. He was never an inspirational speaker. It was all actions. He'd just roll up his sleeves and do the hard stuff, and everyone followed his lead. He's still the best skipper that I've ever been associated with.

LEADERSHIP REFLECTIONS

- Who is a trusted team captain to whom you could give more responsibility?

- How could that person use his or her new duties to maximum effect?

- What are some techniques you could use to increase your focus on whatever "game day" means to you?

PLAYING YOUR BEST WITH A TARGET ON YOUR BACK

In any sport or industry, the best of the best walk around with a target firmly affixed to their backs. When you're at the top of whatever your game is, all your competitors know it. They'll do anything to knock you down so they can take your place. In rugby union, every team the All Blacks face is determined to secure their place in history by besting New Zealand. There's no place to hide. Yet somehow, the All Blacks stay calm under pressure, play their best, and win much more often than not. According to Gill:

> The All Blacks are constantly under pressure, because we're always expected to win. That's what happens when you've won more than 75 percent of your games in over 110 years. The players feel the expectation to win every time they put the black jersey on. It's present for every single minute that you're an All Black. There's no point of shying away from it. Just embrace it, get out there, and do what you do. If you shy away from the pressure, you'll want to just curl up in a little ball. That's not how we do things here. We walk toward the pressure and embrace the challenge every time we step on the park. I love that we're measured by whether we win or not and want that pressure to perform. And then, whether we won or lost, waking up the next day asking, "What can we do better in the next game?"
>
> Our group chases continual success. [After] I've reviewed and critiqued how they played, [I'll] come up

with some ideas for what we can do differently. That's a big part of the challenge and the contest. It's not just the performance, but every little thing that leads up to it. Plus, I want to help people. That combination is what gets me out of bed in the morning. Some of the players talk about waking up and figuring out how they can get closer to being the best in the world, and I'm the same way—I want to try and be one of the best S and C [strength and conditioning] coaches around. That means not just learning from losses, but also taking a long, hard look at wins and thinking, *How can we be even better next week?*

LEADERSHIP REFLECTIONS

- What can you do to help your group thrive under pressure?

- When you face a significant challenge, how do you embrace it rather than flee?

- How can you inspire your team to chase continual success?

CULTIVATING A LIFELONG LOVE OF LEARNING

In addition to being one of the most highly respected strength and conditioning coaches in the world, Gill is also an associate professor of human performance at the University of Waikato. According to his staff profile, "Nic has been combining the role of 'scientist' and 'coach' for over eighteen years." In addition to supervising a group of graduate students each semester, Gill is always on the lookout for information that can allow him to up his game, so that he can help the All Blacks do the same. His research topics include strength and power development, heat acclimation/performing in hot environments, child health and learning, sleep, nutrition, and more.[2] As he said:

> Continually learning is the thing that keeps me invigorated and loving what I do. It doesn't have to be [something] that changes my practice, but could be something that just stimulates my thinking as a coach. That's important, because it ensures that what I'm doing doesn't become stale and boring. I want to make sure I'm growing just as much as the athletes are growing. My wife and I were discussing my role this morning, and I said, "I'm not like them."
>
> She replied, "Yes, you are."
>
> I suppose what she was getting at is that I might not be the one out there on a Saturday, but I'm still very competitive. I relish the challenge, want to win at what I do, and strive to put the players in a position to excel. It has nothing to do with money: I like pushing myself to try and be better than I was last year, because it's a privilege to be in this role as part of a winning group.
>
> I've been coaching since sports went fully professional in New Zealand fifteen or sixteen years ago and have witnessed a lot of change during this time. The All Blacks' previous two strength and conditioning coaches had been with the team for a total of eight years, and I've done the rest since they moved on. A

big part of my longevity with the team is the excellence of the players and coaching staff—they're all winners. Yet if I was just doing the same things as when I started, the players would have surpassed my abilities long ago.

So, I keep seeking out people who can teach me new things and inspire me to keep upping my game. One of them is Christian Cook, who has done a lot of pioneering research into athletes' hormonal responses. Another is [physical therapist, author, and speaker] Kelly Starrett, who has taught me so much about mobility and movement quality and is always seeking out new ways to help athletes perform and recover.

While the All Blacks are recognized as leaders in global sport, one thing that makes the team unique is that they don't have a big backroom staff but prefer to stay lean throughout the organization. According to Gill, this means that he is every bit as hands-on with the players today as he was when he first joined the team all those years ago.

I have an assistant and a physiotherapist who I work closely with, and we're all at every session. If we have a squad of thirty-two players, I work with all of them every day. My assistant often takes the lead with monitoring, and the physio is doing her thing, but I'm actively involved in everything. I previously worked at a club where I had four interns and three assistants. Because I had so many people helping, I never knew exactly what each player was doing or what they had been told, and so I spent most of my time managing staff versus coaching athletes.

Whereas now, I know every single thing about every single player I have with me. I know what they lifted, I know how they're feeling, I know what's sore, I know what running we've got planned this afternoon, and so on. I know everything about every athlete, and really enjoy that intimacy versus me simply managing lots of helpers.

As I've gotten older, something that I've loved more and more is getting away from the laptop and phone and actually getting on the floor. On a typical day, I'm on the training field for three hours, and I'm in the gym for four hours, which is seven hours total that I'm with the athletes. I've probably got the most contact with the players of anyone in the coaching group, and I wouldn't have it any other way.

Communication and building trust are two of the biggest parts of leadership. I try to create an environment in which the players can tell or ask me anything. Some of the younger ones feel a bit unsure of themselves at first because they're used to be being told what to do, so it can take a while for them to feel comfortable opening up. But over time, they see that we're all about being collaborative and open.

Every Monday morning, I'll catch up with each player, find out how he's feeling, and see where his thoughts are for the upcoming week. Then we'll go over what I've planned. Sometimes the player will go with it or he might want to change something. It's important to remember that this is a person—a living organism. So, I have to adapt to what each is thinking, feeling, and doing. Sometimes this doesn't align with where I'm at, so we just keep the dialogue going. It's not about me. It's about us.

LEADERSHIP REFLECTIONS

- What's a new skill you want to learn this year, and what are you going to do to acquire it?

- Who is someone inside or outside your field from whom you could gain wisdom?

- What are some administrative duties you could delegate so you can get down in the trenches with your people more often?

BUILDING WORLD CUP-WINNING TRUST

As a leader, you never want to abdicate responsibility because, as the sign on President Harry Truman's White House desk read, "The buck stops here." You are ultimately responsible for the failure or success of your team. Yet there are times when you must delegate to your troops on the ground and trust them to adapt to changing conditions in a way that will secure the win. At the All Blacks, such a process is never left to chance, but baked into the preparation for each and every game, said Gill:

As a coach, you can't be out there during competition, so it's the leaders of the on-field team who need to be

ready. They're the ones that need to be able to problem-
solve and figure out what's going on, what affects the
target, and how to play in the moment. So, a big part
of the All Blacks' approach is that coaches lead early
in the week and players take over as we get closer to
the performance.

The day before a game, the leaders of the team run
training. The staff have various places they go and sit
to watch. Steve Hansen used to stand and lean on the
left goalpost at the right side of the field every Friday.
[Head coach] Ian Foster would sit up in the stands, and
he'd take the guys who weren't playing that weekend
with him to explain what was going on. The leaders on
the team drive the bus. The closer we get to the game,
the more they take over.

Unlike other sports, in the international rugby union, the
strength and conditioning coach is often on the sideline of
each game. As such, if you watch the documentary film *All
or Nothing: New Zealand All Blacks,* you'll see Gill wearing a
"water" bib over his Adidas warmup jacket and running out
onto the field when a player goes down injured. During this
time, whoever the All Blacks' head coach is (in this series, it
was Steve Hansen, who has since been succeeded by his then
assistant Ian Foster) radios down instructions to Gill to pass
on to the team captains.

The coaches' position in the equivalent of a press box high
up in the stands affords them an elevated view of the action
that isn't available to soccer managers from the dugout or
basketball coaches from the bench. However, with leaders

like Richie McCaw, Kieran Read, Ben Smith, and current captain Sam Cane, such messages aren't always needed for the team to rally and turn a potential defeat into a victory—even on the biggest stage. Gill said:

During the 2011 World Cup, we were at home. We hadn't won the competition for a long time, and we were playing in the final. Though we were winning by eight points to seven, there were only five minutes left and France was throwing everything at us. It was just a brutal contest. I remember hearing our head coach, Graham Henry, screaming down the earpiece with a message he wanted me to deliver because there was a stoppage in the game. So, I ran out on the field and went up to Stephen Donald, Andy Ellis, and Richie McCaw.

The three of them were standing there in a little triangle talking. They were absolutely calm as they discussed how they were going to secure the next scrum. They would plug some holes over here, punch the ball up the middle, move to the right, and kick for the corner. There was no panic, no heavy breathing. They were looking each other in the eye.

There was this eerie calmness, and so I didn't even deliver the message. I didn't need to. I told myself, "Gilly, get out of here—they've got this." And sure enough, they did what they'd planned, and we got across the line to win the game and the World Cup.

FINDING EXTREME BALANCE

When the All Blacks play in the World Cup or head overseas to take on the Springboks in South Africa, the Wallabies in Australia, or the Pumas in Argentina, they can be gone for weeks at a time. As a husband and father of two teenage girls, this can be tough on Gill emotionally. How does he cope? By creating and enforcing strong boundaries for when he's back home with his family. As he said:

> We've got an avocado orchard, and when I finish talking to you, I'll go out and pick up all the prunings. We've just pruned the trees so I'm about to pile all that up to be mulched. It's a beautiful little spot in the country that keeps us sane. When I'm home, I'm home, and when I'm away, I'm away, and so there are really clear periods where I get to take the girls to school or to their sports games. I spend more time with my daughters and wife than my mates who work in normal jobs

in Auckland. It's an extreme balance where I'm either not here or I'm here 24/7.

LEADERSHIP REFLECTIONS

- What's a boundary you need to set or enforce?

- How can you find better balance between your professional and personal lives?

- What can you do to practice being fully present at work and at home?

SUMMARY

In this chapter, we learned how Nic Gill squeezes every last ounce of performance potential from the All Blacks—in the Rugby World Cup, which they've won twice during his tenure; in tours against the British Lions and other teams eager to dethrone the kings of world rugby; and in the bitterly contested Bledisloe Cup against their nemesis, Australia. Behind the team's unprecedented success lies Nic Gill's leadership, which includes empowering his players, rallying after a defeat, finding opportunities in setbacks, playing under pressure, and shaping a culture of consistent excellence.

CHAPTER 5

ON THE CUTTING EDGE

You might think that you're the boss, but if you don't respect your team members, it's harder for them to respect you. So, I think just showing respect for even the lowliest member of the team—whether there's a medical student in the room observing or whatever—is a hallmark of a great leader.

—KATRINA FIRLIK, MD, *Neurosurgeon and Cofounder of HealthPrize Technologies*

One of the most significant problems in healthcare today is medication non-adherence. That was what prompted Katrina Firlik to found Health-Prize Technologies, where today she is chief medical officer. Before this, Firlik was a neurosurgeon in private practice at Greenwich Hospital in Greenwich, Connecticut, and on the clinical faculty at Yale University School of Medicine, as well as author of *Another Day in the Frontal Lobe: A Brain Surgeon Exposes Life on the Inside.*[1]

What kind of leader do you respect? What kind of leader are you? What kind of leader do you want to become? In this chapter with neurosurgeon Katrina Firlik, we hear firsthand what it means to hold life and death in your hands, and how even for this superbly skilled professional, there is a thrill from being part of a team. We see also how, according to Firlik, lifelong learning is important, and leadership comes ultimately from knowing yourself. As she said:

I think there's one particular memory I'll always have of the chairman of neurosurgery when I was training. His name was Peter Jannetta, and he was world famous for trigeminal neuralgia, a form of disabling facial pain. People would come from all over the world to the University of Pittsburgh. Many VIPs would show up at this clinic. They still do, even though he's passed away, because he trained a number of people to do this technique. As a second-year resident, [I was] the lowest person on the totem pole. [I] would be assigned to do the evaluation on a patient in the clinic and then present them to Dr. Jannetta. He would then explain the operation to the patient.

What was interesting, and what I loved about him, which I thought was a great leadership quality, was that even though he was this world-famous neurosurgeon, he truly respected everybody's role on the team, even me as a second-year. For example, a VIP might say: "Dr. Jannetta, I understand that it's a teaching institution. But I don't want any residents. I don't want them training on my case. I don't want anyone in the operating room as a trainee."

Many people would say that. Dr. Jannetta, to his leadership credit, he got that question all the time. He would say, "Our stellar success rates are based on our team approach. And I quote you that because that's what we do in every case. And we don't make exceptions. If we made exceptions, I don't know what our success rate would be."

And he would say that in front of the lowly resident in the room with him. It [gave] a great sense that he really respected [us] in [our] role in the operating room. And our role was—and it sounds crazy—but we called ourselves the can openers. Because [we] were the first in the operating room with a patient, whether it was a VIP or not. And [our] goal was simply to do the first few steps of the operation, which means that [we] position the patient, make the incision, and then the small hole in the skull behind the ear that was required for this operation. At that point, [I] would stop and call the attending surgeon, whether it was Dr. Jannetta or one of his partners.

A MINDFULNESS MOMENT

To rise to the challenge, whether it is sports, crisis management, or surgery, there is the moment of quiet before one steps in. Again and again, we see how elite athletes, winning coaches, and tested professionals take a brief moment to prepare mentally for the intense focus they need in the task ahead. Here is how Firlik describes that moment:

I can't say that I had a specific routine, but something that's common, I think, among a lot of surgeons occurs during the preparation for surgery. Literally, when you're just at the scrub sink washing your hands, it's a time to reflect. And assuming you do a good job, it should be a good few minutes that you're standing there washing your hands and scrubbing your nails. The water's going on and off. It's almost a meditative moment, even though it's a very simple one, where you're about to go into the operating room and get "gowned and gloved" and ready for the case.

For me—and I think most surgeons would echo this—when you're washing your hands right outside the operating room, that's the moment when you are just quieting your mind. Maybe you're going through what your thoughts are, details about the patient. And that's the most obvious point of mental preparation.

There's a lot more that goes on way beforehand when you're planning the operation, planning the approach, planning the options. But the hand-washing at the scrub sink is the most immediate and meditative.

Today, team projects are the norm in corporate environments. Leaders must communicate with a team of experts, support staff, and even clients. What is your communication strategy in a high-pressure environment? Do leaders need to shout, or can they communicate sharply and directly, but not harshly? We asked Firlik how one communicates in a high-pressure environment.

Well, that's a great question, because that was something I was very keen on observing and learning, especially during my training. I saw so many different styles, some that I thought worked really well and some that I hated. But obviously, as you can imagine, with surgical personalities, there's a lot of ego. And some surgeons lose their temper very quickly. Some, even on the extreme end, have thrown instruments if they're mad. It can get ridiculous. And they swear. I don't think that's helpful, even though it does get people to snap to attention. But then on the other hand, more effective surgeons are those that you simply respect because of their skill and their leadership. They don't have to speak loudly or quickly. They don't have to swear. They don't have to yell.

Regarding my own personal style as a surgeon, I hope others would say it was one of mutual respect where I have acted as boss, but more as part of a team. When something needs to be dealt with very quickly, or you need someone to rush out of the operating room and grab an instrument that you don't have in the room, you have to do it firmly. So, to a particular person, you must firmly say what you need. And often it's a series of things. So, you'll say, "Anesthesia, I need you to do this." Address them by name, obviously. Then, "Scrub nurse, I need this." And, "Circulating nurse, I need this." You just very firmly but calmly list your needs.

But, again, I found many different kinds of leadership style, from surgeons who do the yelling and screaming to others who exhibit the calm yet forceful listing of immediate needs from other team members. And I obviously liked the latter, which I tried to emulate.

FINDING YOUR OWN BEST

A consistent theme from the leaders we have met is that their leadership developed over time. The leader of today may not be the same person as when he or she began the leadership journey. Initially, many leaders emulated their mentors and teachers. Then, with experience, confidence, and training, they found their own best set. Where are you in your development as a leader? Here, Firlik discusses her style:

> I don't naturally like bossing people around. It's not one of my childhood traits, and so the idea of telling people what to do—which is part of the job—came more gradually during training as I realized, okay, obviously I need to tell people what to do. I'm the one in charge of the operation or the one in charge in the office evaluating a patient. So, I think that comes with learning the ropes and what every team member's role is. And I think I probably learned that most efficiently when I was called to a trauma in the emergency room, which is something we frequently do as a surgeon.
>
> Serious trauma cases are dramatic examples where everybody has their role. Let's say it's a car accident victim. There might be multiple injuries, orthopedic injuries, or head injuries, and everybody's rushing to the emergency room at the same time. You have your orthopedic surgeon and neurosurgeon, and everybody understands their roles based on the hierarchy of injuries. And then there's the emergency room doctors, the paramedic dropping off the patient, and usually two or three nurses. It's a complex team working together at a fast pace.
>
> It's truly amazing when you have a well-oiled machine like that, and everybody understands their role. And when each individual steps into that role, there's often very little conversation. It's a really thrilling thing to be a part of, when everybody is almost

wordlessly going about their business. In my mind, that's the most memorable example of being on a team—in a trauma case where seconds count, everybody steps up, knowing when to come in and when to get out of the way. It's a wonderful process to be a part of.

When we talk about being "in the zone," it's often in reference to athletics. However, as Firlik describes, the complex interactions between elite team members on a surgical crew can also bring about this euphoria. The countless hours of practice and repetition with teammates bring about an almost mystical level of intuitive mental and physical collaboration, she says.

That absolutely is the case where sometimes things are going so smoothly that it's almost like it's happening on its own, and that typically happens in operations that you've done dozens or maybe even hundreds of times. You do them so often that you fall into a nice routine. But then obviously sometimes things go wrong. The patient's anatomy is slightly different than the vast majority. Or there's a blood vessel that you don't typically encounter that requires you to spend ten minutes stopping the bleeding. Also, I think, . . . whether or not there is that flow depends on the team.

For example, during an operation, you have a surgeon with a scrub nurse, who's actually scrubbed in with a surgeon handing her instruments, then there's a circulating nurse who's out and about, grabbing things and so on. What's interesting is when you're with a

scrub nurse whom you've worked with many times
on the same operation. You almost don't even have to
speak, because the nurse will be looking at the screen,
so that she or he sees what you're seeing under the
microscope and will simply hand you the right instrument at the right time without you even making a
verbal request.

When I can put my hand out to the nurse without
even saying what instrument to put into it, because
she's watching the screen and is experienced as well,
that's what helps lead to the flow state. . . .

That's probably the best example of a flow state. It's
not only doing a procedure that's so familiar with you,
but also working with someone that's been there with
you before. On the other hand, there are other cases
where maybe somebody's new or [doesn't] know what
instruments you like or, again, like I mentioned, the
patient's anatomy is slightly different or the tumor acts
like it shouldn't. You thought it was going to be a soft
tumor and, all of a sudden, it's extremely hard and it's
stuck to everything, and it takes you three times the
amount of time. That can get very frustrating, and you
don't feel like you're in a flow state, but you just have
to calm yourself down and work at it.

Surgeons love that. It's exciting. It's almost calm-
ing to be in a scenario where everybody's working
together, everybody knows what they're doing, and
it's a seamless flow state.

As Firlik mentions, sometimes an operation doesn't go
smoothly or is very arduous. As with any situation in life,

it is not the smooth and easy tasks that challenge us, but rather the unexpected and the unusual. In describing surgery, she mentions how the team works together to get through a lengthy operation, where just one person is not going to be able to complete it on their own. In the following account, you'll hear echoes of similar characteristics that define superior teamwork. For example, Tammie Jo Shults describes the teamwork between her and her copilot as they dealt with an unfolding crisis, and Nick Peters describes how he motivated his crews through brush fires. Firlik adds:

> The truth is that during a long operation—typically tumor operations where a very complex tumor is in a very difficult part of the brain—there are multiple steps to the operation. Obviously, you have to be focused the whole time, but that critical focus, where you're almost holding your breath because you're dealing with millimeters of accuracy, is not required for the entire operation. There are many long periods, usually in the opening and the closing, that could account for the vast majority of the time. So, in those long operations, ones that last for hours, there's almost never a single surgeon, because physiologically you can't either sit or stand or look through a microscope for that long.
>
> You often tag team, where . . . the senior surgeon [does] the bulk of the work, but then [goes] out to the lounge and uses the bathroom and gets a bite to eat and then his or her partner will step in for a while and work on the tumor. And especially in a teaching hospital, you might have the residents doing the

so-called easier part of the case, the opening and the closing. For example, once the tumor is out, it might be another two hours or more to actually close it up because everything's done in layers. That part is critical but doesn't require the same laser-like focus that is required under the microscope. But it does require long hours of stitching and closing layers, and that's when you might even turn the music on. Then people are more relaxed, and it's the more routine part of the operation.

GRATITUDE AND THE PRIVILEGE OF LEARNING

A significant part of leadership, and especially of senior leadership, is the responsibility to have a succession plan and a way to mentor and educate the next generation. Strong confident leaders are often those most willing to share and pass on their knowledge. Do you carve out time to bring others up? Are there institutional processes to build and retain knowledge capital as Firlik describes? Firlik describes here the value of learning:

> I think this is just part of my personality. One of the reasons I started a company is that I love learning to do new things. During your surgical training, you're on a very steep part of the learning curve the entire time. You're learning new operations and the mastery of technique, which is really exciting. In the beginning, you're relegated to just watching, and then you're able to do a little bit to help. And then finally you're able to do something on your own, but it's a very long process.

That's how safety is maintained. But I loved being on that steep part of the learning curve where, every day, it's a new case or new operation. It was thrilling to see different surgeons' techniques, different ways of accomplishing something in the operating room, which was also fascinating.

Some surgeons were amazing at teaching surgical technique. As a resident, I could have the instruments in my hand, my mentor would be talking through what the moves are, and I would feel like I was operating through him. But then other surgeons were not very good at that, and they would take the instruments out of my hand because they were so frustrated. They had trouble describing what the next move was going to be, so I didn't get to learn as much. I loved seeing that diversity of styles and being on the steep part of the learning curve.

One of the most gratifying parts of becoming a surgeon during residency is that you go through different phases. In your seventh year, you're the chief resident in charge of all the other residents. And then when you're out in practice, you're your own boss. But it is thrilling to see something through a new resident's eyes, [who is] seeing an operation for the first time. You can sense the wonder, but then you're also helping to give [the resident] confidence. A very common procedure that we would do, not in the operating room, but at the bedside for trauma patients, would be to drill a small hole in the skull with a little handheld drill kit that you open right there in the ICU. It's called placing an external ventricular drain, or EVD.

And that's something junior residents had to learn to do pretty quickly. I taught countless residents how to do that at the bedside. Watching [others] learn and become proficient was really thrilling to me, because you see their confidence building, teaching them to do it calmly, and allowing them to do it rather than doing it yourself. That does require some trust in them and fortitude on your own part to give the reins over. But seeing that proficiency develop within a trainee is really exciting.

Along with mentoring, training, and leading, many leaders mention the importance of finding balance and respite. Nick Peters mentioned that he would go home after a fire and tell his wife, "I'm not making a decision for three days." As we'll see in Chapter 6, Coach Paul Ratcliffe finds relaxation by spending time with his family. Similarly, Katrina Firlik mentions pursuing her hobbies and a need to prepare for life after a career.

In surgery—and especially neurosurgery—it was hard to have a lot of balance. A lot of surgeons talked about their family being resentful because their patients had to come first, which is often the simple reality. But in terms of positive examples, I've always gravitated toward surgeons who had a sense of humor and outside hobbies. I think that's important because you're only a surgeon for so long, and if you end up retiring in your sixties, you need a life outside of that. And a lot of surgeons' lives fall apart once they retire. I think a great example is surgeons who have hobbies on the side that they at least try to do whenever they can, whether it's traveling or fly-fishing or cycling. And that was gratifying for me to see because, okay, I could understand that there's a life outside of the operating room. You have to kind of force yourself to continue those hobbies because they're critical, not just during your surgical career, but even more so afterward.

For me, just going outside and taking long walks is my number one [way to unwind]. That's always been my favorite activity—just walking. Doing anything outdoors is almost a trite example, but it definitely works for me. More recently, cooking has become really important to me. I enjoy the procedural nature of it. It reminds me of being in the operating room and doing the opening, the heart of the case, and then the closing. Cooking in many ways mirrors an operation. And just like in surgery, you then get the excitement of seeing the end result, which is hopefully a good one, but not always.

YOUR BEST EFFORT MEANS BEST TEAM EFFORT

Continuing with several themes that are brought up repeatedly by exceptional leaders, Firlik highlights the importance of respecting every team member. We could see this when President Barack Obama paused for a moment before a big speech to acknowledge a White House staff member. Or when Rafael Nadal takes the time to greet and thank the ball boys and girls at the French Open. Almost without exception, those performing and working at the highest levels continue to respect and acknowledge the support of those around them. According to Firlik:

> Just as it was important to respect every member of my surgical team, it's critical to acknowledge every person in a business organization. I was cofounder of Health-Prize Technologies and am still chief medical officer. I was there from day one, conceived the idea of the company, and then helped to make our first hires. In my company, we picked our team members, whereas often with surgery, you're put with people that the hospital or someone else hired. In both business and medicine, I learned not to micromanage because you really do have to respect everybody's role. Even if their role is something you consider to be a smaller one, because then I think they'll work harder knowing that they're being respected in that way.

As Firlik moved from neurosurgery to the role of entrepreneur at her start-up, she was challenged with the need to acquire new knowledge, skills, and experience. This included providing day-to-day management, growing a sustainable company, understanding the financials, and learning to deal with venture capitalists. How does a leader, who is skilled at the highest level in a field, transition and learn in new situations? Here is how Firlik responded to that question:

> I think that humility comes into play. You have to ask a lot of questions and not be scared to ask something that might come across as dumb. Luckily, because I had the neurosurgery background, people aren't

necessarily reacting to a "dumb" question with, "Okay, this is a dumb person." They're thinking, "Okay, this is a neurosurgeon learning something new." So, that made it a bit easier. But, still, I did have a lot of mentors. I was constantly asking my cofounder questions, but if it was something simple like confusion over a new acronym, I would quickly do the work myself and look it up. When it came to finding answers to more complex strategy questions like, "How can we decide which people we need to hire and at what stages?" the answers came from asking a lot of people.

Luckily, my husband is a venture capitalist (by way of surgery first), and so I was able to learn a lot through him, but also from people I met who were seasoned entrepreneurs. So, just learning from other cofounders and CEOs of start-up companies, asking a lot of questions, going out for lunch, and picking their brain. That was really the goal, especially in the first year. But I spent a number of months learning before I even cofounded the company. A big part of that was just learning the ropes and understanding the lingo.

I think you have to have a lot of humility, especially in the beginning, because even though my company is in healthcare, I was not even familiar with a lot of the acronyms that would be thrown around in investor meetings or when we were dealing with the financial side of the industry. I had to rapidly learn a lot of these things, which is actually what I craved at that stage of my career. Again, as I mentioned, I love being on a steep learning curve. So the challenge of starting and building a company was one I was looking forward to. But you do need to have the humility to learn new things and to realize foremost—especially when you're changing careers like this—that you're not the expert. You may be the expert at certain aspects. So, as chief medical officer, the medical angle was my expertise, but you have to respect the expertise of the financial person and the executives with more managerial skills than you have.

Starting a company was exciting because I got to figure out, "How do I become a better manager?" "How do I understand how to look at the balance sheet?" "When I'm pitching to an investor, what are the questions I'm going to ask?" And when I became proficient at that, it reminded me of being a resident again. What I most loved about being a resident was learning new things. Then, in starting a company, I learned to have a conversation with a potential investor and answer his or her questions so that they were satisfied with my understanding of the finances. For some reason, that was just thrilling to me: becoming proficient in something that was not my area of expertise.

There is a recurring theme from many of our leaders featured in this book: be true to yourself. To be exceptional, you must develop into the leader you want to be. Although all leaders are shaped by those around them in their formative years and by mentors, coaches, and teachers, it is important to learn and choose the best parts that fit your personality, character, and outlook. What are your strengths? Where do you shine? Here, Firlik describes being true to herself:

I think it's important to have the confidence to allow your own personality to shine through. For example, if you find yourself in a very male-dominated profession. I think some of the older women, some of the first women in surgery, tended to act a little more masculine, because that was the traditional way you wielded power—to take on more traditional male characteristics. Not until recently have there been more women in the field, so now it's more accepted to act more like a woman. Obviously, these are stereotypes we're talking about, because not all women act the same nor do all men act the same, but you know what I'm talking about. It's okay to act more openly feminine as a surgeon or as a leader, and it won't hopefully be seen as being weak.

WHO DO LEADERS LOOK TO?

What's in your leadership toolbox? Are you a details-focused person? Do you tackle broader issues and strategies? How do you engage with peers as well as those with smaller roles on the team? How do you convey respect to others? Do you initiate activities that increase engagement and develop talent? And how do you go about doing all this? Firlik mentions an example from some of the newer leaders on the world stage who received plaudits for their adept actions and leadership during the COVID-19 pandemic:

Lately, I've been following the prime minister of New Zealand, Jacinda Ardern. I don't have a lot of experience in following female leaders, especially a young leader with a new baby. This is such a rare example. Her empathy comes across very strongly. Although there are certainly plenty of men with amazing empathy, hers seems to come across in a particularly female way that I think is neat to observe. That's a more recent example that I can think of where I'm keenly following what she says, following her tweets and that sort of thing, because I love watching her.

Basically, she acts very "womanly" as a leader. You know, some of the older women in the operating room would swear or act rough with others. That might have been their native personality, but it also may have been that they felt they needed to take on that personality to fit into that role. I think in the modern era, you can be yourself—you don't have to put on airs of what the typical leader looks like, feels like, and acts like. I aim to emulate that freedom. You should be comfortable in your own personality. Whether you're a woman, or gay, or an ethnic minority, or no matter what your background is, it should be okay to be your natural self. Act as your own person and be a leader that way, as opposed to trying to figure out what the typical leader looks and acts like.

Almost all the leaders profiled in this book mention challenges they encountered that forged their outlook and approach. How you handle challenges and how you respond to someone who challenges you are pivot points as you become a leader. You may be a pilot who gets to know the flight crew and builds trust by helping to clean dirty seats. You may be a fire crew leader who understands the fears of each rookie and veteran alike, and knows what to say at the edge of a fire break. You may be a coach who respects the time of your student athletes. Or, as Firlik says, you may be a neurosurgeon exposed to different and sometimes off-putting cultural perspectives and biases:

> I think [it is important to have] a sense of humor. I don't mean by just telling jokes, but more by having a sense of levity, which is really critical. I've seen unfortunate examples in neurosurgery in particular where a female neurosurgery resident heard an off-color comment by an older surgeon and processed it in such a way that both parties ended up suffering needlessly.
>
> I heard my share of questionable comments myself, but I chalked them up to a culture conflict, and such conflicts take time to change. In fact, I majored in cultural anthropology, and I'm fascinated by such conflicts. For example, when I was a medical student interviewing for neurosurgery positions, one of the interviewers, who was probably in his fifties and of Middle Eastern background, said, "How do you know you can handle a surgical drill?" He looked at me, and I'm relatively short and not at all muscular. Clearly, he was honestly concerned that I might not be able to handle the drill.
>
> But I didn't take it personally. Instead I just muttered something like, "You'll just have to accept me to see how I can handle a drill."

Again, I studied cultural anthropology, which was actually my first love, so I'm fascinated by different cultures. I realized that he had probably never operated with a woman before. And so I felt I had to give him a little bit of leeway. The question could have been seen as inappropriate, but I understood why he was asking it. And the cool thing was that I was accepted by that program, and I got to do a lot of spine cases with him. We worked incredibly well together in the operating room. He's a great guy. We had a great friendship. In fact, when I finished my residency, I was offered a job by his group.

I think it's important to understand cultural differences, especially when you're a young woman working with an older man. It doesn't excuse the comments, and the need for acceptance should go both ways, but it makes such comments more understandable. And then if you can have a sense of humor, an off comment won't ruin your day. And most important, by being a female neurosurgeon, you will help to change the culture over time.

WHEN IT COUNTS

In our sample of leaders, we have chosen several who excelled in life-or-death situations. From firefighting to piloting to brain surgery. What is it that allows these leaders to function in such high-stakes situations? How do you preserve at least a level of calm that is necessary for everyone to do their job and get to the desired outcome rather than allowing panic to set in? Firlik gives us some valuable insight into how this plays out in an operating room.

I think so much depends on tactical proficiency. My training was seven years long. By the time you've gotten through those seven years, you've hopefully at least seen some—well, almost all—of the complications that could occur, whether you were the one taking care of it or your attending [physician] was the one taking charge of it. When you're out on your own, you can think back: "Okay. I've seen this before. When there's a rush of bleeding here at this point in the operation, I know what to do." Because you've practiced it so many times, you're able to draw on that wealth of knowledge and technical proficiency. But, obviously, there is heart rate elevation that occurs and a bit of a panic that sets in for a brief moment.

But then you quickly go to your reserves of knowledge and technical proficiency. It requires taking a deep breath. The other team members in the operating room tend to know what's going on because there's often a screen that everybody can watch to see what's happening under the microscope.

For example, during brain surgery, if all of a sudden there's a rush of blood that fills the screen, the nurses, the anesthesiologists, everyone realizes, "Okay, that's not good." And everyone's quiet. You may allow yourself only a brief moment of panic and then take a deep breath before you draw from your well of cognitive and technical proficiency.

SUMMARY

This chapter took a deep dive into the mind and life of a neurosurgeon. Through an account of what it is like inside the surgical suite and what it takes to transition from doctor to chief medical officer of a start-up, Katrina Firlik touched upon many themes that have come up again and again from exceptional leaders: the need to learn and develop your own style, the importance of respecting everyone on the team because you will need to depend on them to succeed, the necessity of finding balance or at least an outside hobby, and the beauty of the moment just before you get in the zone, when you "allow yourself only a brief moment of panic and then take a deep breath."

CHAPTER 6

SHAPING FUTURE LEADERS

What I try to do is identify my strongest leaders on the team. We have them put down on a piece of paper all the values that they want from their team, from all the student athletes. They go through all the things that are important to them, and then that becomes our culture.

—PAUL RATCLIFFE, *Head Coach, Stanford Cardinal Women's Soccer*

Paul Ratcliffe is the most successful coach in more than a hundred years of Stanford soccer, among men or women. In his seventeen seasons as head coach, Ratcliffe has never failed to direct the Cardinal to the NCAA tournament. He is Stanford's winningest soccer coach, with a 320-52-29 record. Under his leadership, the Stanford women won three national championships, reached five NCAA finals, won nine Pac-12 titles, played in nine College Cups, and reached the NCAA third round in thirteen of the past fourteen seasons. The Cardinal has advanced to the College Cup in nine of the past twelve seasons. Ratcliffe is an eight-time Pac-12 Coach of the Year. No other Pac-12 coach has won more than twice in the history of the conference. He is a three-time NSCAA National Coach of the Year.[1]

Leaders often loom larger than life. They inspire, motivate, and move us forward. But where do they come from? Is leadership an innate gift? Is it acquired through training in an MBA program or the ROTC? Is it something we can develop in ourselves? Coaches specialize in identifying, developing, and bringing out leadership. What makes some coaches better than others?

PEOPLE WHO INFLUENCE YOU

When looking at the background of leaders, there is often a strong figure or a set of them. This can be a parent, coach, mentor, or other role model. What is interesting about Ratcliffe's account is that he mentions the dynamic between his own father and mother as formative. Such a theme rings true for many leaders. According to Coach Ratcliffe, his family's influence left an indelible mark:

> You're shaped by all of the people that you've been influenced by. My dad is a very strong leader, has a lot of leadership abilities, and is a driven person. I'm from the North of England, originally Leeds. He was from the North of England. He was in the army, and so he always gave me that strong work ethic and no messing around, get to business, get things done. I think I really learned a lot from him.
>
> He became a tailor in the army, and then went on to be a sales rep in the clothing trade. He was just a go-getter. He would get up early in the morning and go after it and get his job done. And just a very determined personality and person.
>
> The best way to describe him is that he was a self-starter. And I think if you're going to be a leader, you have to be a self-starter, you have to be ambitious, and you have to get after it. He was like that. I don't

think he was trying to teach me things; it was just how he was as a person. And as a kid, you're picking up [everything] from your parents, all their habits. He had really good habits that I think I've picked up, which has helped me become a good coach.

Obviously my mom was influential in my life, too. She was a great example of really caring about people and understanding where they're coming from. With my parents, it's interesting. I think my mom was very laid back and nurturing: "Oh, don't worry. Take a day off school, relax, and enjoy yourself."

And my dad would be like, "You have to go to school every damn day, and get there and get stuff done." You know what I mean?

I had the two extremes, which was interesting growing up. You have the one that's highly motivated pushing you, and the other one's saying you need a break, it's good for your mental health, just relax, take it easy.

I think it was good for me, because it made me consider as I got older, which one do I want to be? Do I want to be relaxed and not worry about anything and just have a peaceful, good life? Or do I want to be driven and achieve things and get after it? And I think my conclusion was I want to do both. How can I do that? Work really hard when you're on and be assertive and get after it. But also realize you do need a break sometimes, and you need to spend some time with your family and get away from things. I think I was really fortunate to have two parents that were different.

Ratcliffe also mentions his own coaches as he was growing up. He notes that although coaches give you a target, a model, and a perspective, ultimately, one must develop and choose what suits oneself best. He says:

> My college coach Ziggy Schmidt was a great role model for me—very demanding, but really a good person. I've been lucky enough to have had so many good coaches.
>
> Actually, I had coaches in the past that had that [demanding, strict] style. I have to bring elements of that, because sometimes you do have to be a hard leader with people, and you have to be strong. But that's not going to be my leadership type or style. I think just being true to yourself, who you are as a person, and finding people to help you be a leader, to bring out your strengths that complement you, because there's no perfect person or perfect leader. I've yet to see one. I think it's very hard to be perfect. You just have to realize that and be the best you can be for your student athletes.
>
> I think when you put all these things together, that's the person you are and that's the type of leader you're going to be. It's really important to realize that you're being shaped by everyone around you. You've got to take the best of all those people and put them into focus if you want to be successful.

CREATING CULTURE

What is it exactly that leaders do? They're usually not the
best at everything. For example, no soccer coach actually
plays better than Lionel Messi or Carli Lloyd. The coach
might not even be the smartest person in the organization.
So, what is leadership? Ratcliffe says that part of his job is
to create a culture that comes from all the individuals and
components within his influence:

> The difficult part of being a coach is creating culture.
> The one thing I've done that I think has been the most
> powerful thing is to create a good culture. A strong
> culture doesn't come from just the head coach, it comes
> from the entire team. What I try to do is identify my
> strongest leaders on the team. We have them put down
> on a piece of paper all the values that they want from
> their team, from all the student athletes. They go
> through all the things that are important to them, and
> then that becomes our culture. That sets our attitudes,
> that sets our mentality and all the values they want to
> have as a team. And then they have accountability and
> ownership, because they created that. It's their team,
> it's their culture, and they create it.
>
>   It's not just Paul Ratcliffe's culture. It's Stanford
> women's soccer culture. It comes from all of us and,
> most important, from our student athletes. I think,
> implicitly, they're going to really buy into that because
> it's their culture. I think that's the most important
> thing that I've done to create that strong culture. And I

think, within it, the most important thing is just knowing that all of the student athletes trust each other, care about each other, want to play for each other, and don't want to let each other down.

That's the kind of culture I want to create—where people show up to training and you owe it to your teammates to give maximum effort, because we want this to be a positive experience for everyone and want to achieve our goal. Our goal might be to get to the national championship and win that game, and every day we've got to give maximum effort. And that means that even if you're having a tough day or things aren't going right for you, you got to find that energy to do it for your teammates and not just for you.

The [key to] leadership with my student athletes is just communicating with them. And I'm really fortunate because, at Stanford, I attract future leaders, not just in athletics, but also in the world, in academics, in business, and in everything. I'm really lucky to get kids with strong leadership abilities when they come to me, and it's just bringing out the best in them and making sure they know that I believe in them. I care about them, and I want them to be successful.

I think a lot of communication comes down to observation. You have to observe what that team needs and then talk to your leaders about what we need to address and make sure you're emphasizing that. Every year it can change. For me it changes with what I think is important.

What steps and messages do you convey to create a specific culture? Do you identify individuals who will lead the team? Are you careful in observing a situation to make an accurate and decisive evaluation?

Ratcliffe emphasizes that, in the culture he is nurturing, it is vital to have trust in one another. It is necessary that all team members put in total effort so as not to let one another down. He also mentions that the culture is not necessarily entirely of his own making; it comes from athletes that he identifies as leaders on the team. This may answer the question of what it is that leaders actually do. The best leader brings out maximum possible effort and outcomes from a team, organization, or even a nation of people through the culture that they develop.

TELLING TRAITS

Do strong leaders show typical characteristics? What indicators suggest the potential to develop into an effective leader? Ratcliffe talks about general character traits and also work ethic. He is not looking for someone who is boasting about a success or filled with alpha ego. Instead, as he describes here, he's quite clear that he is looking for the ability to grow, a willingness to reflect upon each day, and the dedication to work to get better.

The most important thing for me when I'm looking for staff would be trust, because you have to find people that you know you really can rely on and will not be doing anything behind your back to hurt the team's chances. We all have to be on the same page as coaches. Trust will be the number one thing for us.

There are so many other things I look for. The most important I would hope for is integrity and honesty: they're a good human being first, and they care about their student athletes. Also, a strong work ethic, that they realize you have to work hard if you want to be successful. You have to be willing to grind and put in the hours. And then, ultimately, passion for the game. I really love the game, and my hope is that they, too, love the game and get enjoyment out of it as well.

The thing you hope is that they reflect on you as a coach, and they say: "Hey, he had a really good perspective. He taught me the game at the highest level, but he was a great human being and really cared about me." Ultimately, I think that's the most important thing.

And when it comes to players, I think I'm looking for character. You know, how strong in character are they? Are they going to be good teammates? Do they have a strong work ethic? Are they intelligent? Will they be coachable? All those things are important because you have to have them in the right frame of mind to be able to mold them into great players. If they're selfish and don't care about others and things like that, it's going to be hard to get through to them and help them grow as players. And then, obviously, I'm looking at their ability, their talent level, their athleticism, and all those other factors. But the most important thing I would say is just their overall character, that they're a good person, they're competitive, they want to work hard, and they're intelligent.

I look for little things, like if they're bad-mouthing a previous coach or a previous manager they had, as that might be a red flag. It's not my style to say negative things about people in the past. It's just not how I work. I think a lack of work ethic or the desire to get better and improve would be red flags to me. . . . I would just have to read them a little bit, get to know them, and chat with them.

Something I've always thought about as a coach— and I have friends who have been very successful outside of coaching that have asked me about this, too—is "What do you ask student athletes when they come into your office to decipher whether they're going to be a good recruit for you?" That's so difficult to answer. I haven't come up with a key question, but I've always thought, *What could it be?*

Sometimes I ask, "What do you attribute your success to?" And I'm hoping they're not going to say, "Oh, it's just because I had a great coach." I'm hoping it's going to be more like, "It's because I'm passionate about the game, I work hard at it, and I want to be the best I can be."

They're not going to attribute it to outside forces like, "I got lucky," or "I'm just a great athlete." It's more like, "I really work hard at it, and I want to get better." I'm looking for athletes who have the capacity to continue to grow, because sometimes I get them at eighteen [and] they might be tapped out. I don't want that. I want them to be a future pro player, hopefully, or have potential to be a future pro player. At eighteen, you don't want them satisfied or thinking, "I'm good because it just happened." It's because, "Every day I want to grow and get better."

Ratcliffe reflects on young leaders of today. Despite all the accoutrements of wealth that are typical for many of the students attending Stanford University, Ratcliffe doesn't think that this generation is necessarily more spoiled than those of the past. Leaders today, just as in the past, show grit, mental toughness, and a work ethic to get what they're looking for and achieve their goals. He says:

I think the one thing I would say is that life is getting easier for kids. My concern is that any time I've had success, *perseverance* is the word that comes to mind. You have to persevere through setbacks and through difficult times and really push yourself to the brink to get to that achievement that you want. It's harder for kids to get to that point than it was in the past, but we have to get back to that, because if you truly want to be great, you have to push yourself. But in saying that, I'm very fortunate at Stanford, as I think I attract a lot of those kids that are willing to put in the hard work, and they are doing it.

I've had so many kids that have really impressed me through the years, that really have that work ethic. But the ones who get to the top that I've coached— that move on to the national team—they have that grit, that determination, that work ethic that you're looking for, that mental toughness that's critical to being successful.

WINNING

Winning is ultimately the metric that is counted in athletics. Ironically, as one of the winningest coaches of all time, Ratcliffe doesn't really focus on that quantitative measurement. Instead, he says, he looks for chemistry, the right combination of players, and day-to-day effort to get better, all while enjoying the effort.

We don't talk about it. I don't think the players would want me to talk about it. It's more about trying to meet our potential as a group, trying to find the right chemistry, the right combinations of players on the field, and working as hard as we can and to give ourselves the possibility of competing for the championship. But you can't just talk about a championship. Then they get carried away. It's a process and it's a journey to get to that point. For me, it's day to day: How can we get better each and every day and really enjoy the journey of getting to that point? Then hopefully we get an opportunity to compete for a championship, but we're going to have to earn it.

I think that it's a little different when you're coaching in college, because I get a cycle of players graduating and new players coming in. So, sometimes I get frustrated with that, because just when you've gotten the players to where you really want them to be mentally and focus-wise, they're graduating. You want the older players to relay those messages to the younger ones, because there are so many great lessons learned from not being successful and from losing, which I think is when you learn the most. But when you weigh in, it's very hard to win back-to-back because everyone's on a cloud and saying, "Hey, we're good." And sometimes they don't work quite as hard as they should.

It's always a challenge. For me as a coach, I would say you're only as good as your last game. And as soon as you lose, everything changes. No one's smiling or glowing or saying, "Hey, we're pretty good." It's all: "We've got to get better. We've got to roll up our sleeves. What can we do to improve?" I think that athletics keeps you humble, because every once in a while, you're going to lose, even if you're the greatest team. And that's going to keep you honest and make you realize that you've got to work hard.

This year, we had one loss before we won the championship. That loss was the greatest thing that could happen to us because it gave me a chance to address the team, the importance of determination and grit and work ethic, and not just [winning] because you're talented. It's how much you put into it on the day. And that really helped us toward the end, that we had that grit and determination, because we learned that lesson from losing that game.

In sports, there is always a winner and a loser. What do champions do when they encounter the inevitable loss? What does a coach say? And what don't they say? Here is how Coach Ratcliffe answers those questions:

> The first thing you don't want to do is to lose your temper straightaway, but you do want to address it quickly. I try to remain as calm as I can and address what happened. Then the next day we can really address it when I'm sure of what I'm saying and when people have calmed down emotionally. Then I'll talk about it. That's the thing I think about—that as a great leader or a great coach, you have to be really good at observing. You have to observe what really went wrong, and you have to be accurate, because if you observe the wrong things or you think the wrong things were the reason for your loss, you can really disrupt and hurt the group and will lose credibility as a coach.
>
> You have to be very careful about how you observe it. Sometimes you have to talk to a lot of the players and say, "Hey, what were your thoughts?" Get a lot of input from people and see what they're thinking were some of the reasons for the poor performance.
>
> But ultimately, they're going to look to you as the leader to tell them definitively, "This was the reason." You have to be really smart about observing the right things and saying the right things after a loss and realizing that people are very sensitive afterward, because they probably still worked hard and put a lot into it, and they're very disappointed that they didn't win. It wasn't like they just showed up and didn't care that day. They always cared—it just didn't go your way.

Sometimes it might be just one of those days. It was just an off day, and you have to tell the team that and say: "Hey, we have to learn from it. It was an off day. People didn't perform." It might've been my fault. I trained them too hard through the week. I have to observe what the real reason was and identify that and make sure I figure it out and I'm accurate with that, in order for us continue to move forward after that setback.

[Before Stanford's national title-winning game] I think I said: "We've worked so hard the whole year to get this opportunity. Let's take advantage of it. Our determination, our hunger, and our drive are going to win through. Trust your teammates, play for each other, and make everyone proud." That's what I said, and I know as a team they got together and talked, too. Other years, I said something like: "Hey, let's take care of business. This is our time. Let's take care of this. Let's finish strong. Let's show what we're made of." You're just trying to inspire them a little bit. You don't want to say too much and get caught up in all the emotion. It's more just, "Go out there and prove something today."

BALANCE AND BOUNDARIES

In almost any leadership position, there are many demands. There are people all around you pulling at your time. How does one find balance? Is it possible? Ratcliffe mentions how his family helps him to regain perspective, rather than just being another demand on his time. Additionally, he says, it's important to him to be available to his players, be respectful of their time, and take into account all the pressures they're dealing with as busy student athletes.

Coaching is a difficult occupation to have a balance in your life and for your family. Because a lot of the weekends are spent on the field when most families are spending time together, you're working your hardest usually as a coach. So, that's always been challenging. But I've always had good perspective. I think I learned it from my dad. He used to work very hard during the day. Then, when he came home, he would turn that off and just spend time with the family and enjoy it. I've tried to do that even though it's hard because I have recruiting calls late at night and different things that come up with coaching that I have to address. But I try my best wherever I go, whatever I do with coaching, and work really hard at it.

And then I want to cut it off, commit some time to my family, and start again on my coaching later and work hard again. It's important to realize that you have to prioritize both those things, because coaching will easily take over your whole life. There's always someone who wants to talk to you about coaching or whatever it is. It's all consuming. And then you have twenty-eight players on your team who want your attention and need your help. There are just so many things going on, but you have to learn to have a balance with your family, which I think is critical, and live your life, too. And it helps me.

Probably one of the greatest things for me was having children. I used to take losses really hard. Then after I had kids, I would lose a game and I'd be down in the dumps, and my kids would run over and jump on me. They didn't know I lost the game. They were little kids. They had no idea. They didn't care. They just saw Dad, and it gave me good perspective that: "Hey, it's just a game I lost. I've got to move on. Learn from it and move on." I don't like that feeling [of losing], but there are more important things. It gave me perspective and balance in life. I think it's crucial to have that.

I don't know if I've set boundaries necessarily, because there are going to be times when I have to make phone calls after hours. It's important, and I'm going to do it. But I try my best to get as much of my job done during the day so that when I go home I can spend some time with my family. But I still will set up phone calls where I say, "At 8:00 p.m., I'm going to have an important call for forty-five minutes."

I don't think there are any boundaries at work. I want to make sure I'm there for all my student athletes and help them as much as possible. It's just a matter of time management, I think, being disciplined with your time management. But it's hard with technology, it's hard to set those boundaries, because people can always get ahold of you. And I want to be respectful of people that if they need to get ahold of me, I want to be able to get ahold of them, too, and talk to them. But it's one of those things in life. You have to do it, but I don't want it to go so far where it dictates my life, I'm always on edge, and I'm never relaxed or hanging out with my family.

I would say just going for a walk is good. I like to stay relatively fit. I'm an active person so I want to get outdoors in the fresh air. But most important, walking for me is good for my mental health. To get outside and just think about my day and things that are going on. And it's a way to relax for me. Listening to music is another good way for me to relax. It's most important, though, to spend time with my kids and my wife. Just being with my family is the best thing.

I think [my student athletes] do a great job, honestly. My big thing is that I want to be very understanding of their time and respectful of it. The thing I demand of them is that when we're training for two hours, let's work very hard, have really good, deliberate, intense sessions, and improve. And then when we're done, you guys get back to your business. I hope they get some time to relax, but also get back to their schoolwork. And they're really good about it. Their time management skills are fantastic. The most important thing is that I'm supportive of them. I encourage them to do well and recognize when they succeed, not just on the field but also in the classroom, recognizing those moments and saying: "Hey, well done. I saw your grades, really proud of you. You're doing an exceptional job. Keep up the good work."

Because then they know you don't just care about them as an athlete, you care about them as a student as well, which I do. And it is hard work to be at Stanford, but it's also an incredible opportunity for all my student athletes. Something I talk to them about a lot is to take full advantage of both—not just the athletic opportunities here, but also the academic opportunities, the networking, and all the things that you can get out of Stanford University. Please take advantage of everything.

LEADERSHIP SELF-REFLECTION QUESTIONS

- How do you reflect and impress on those looking to you for leadership that you respect their time?

- Are mandates just coming from above, or is there bottom-up consensus building and input to develop action plans?

- As a leader, are you giving others every opportunity to take advantage of your organization's resources?

THE PILLARS OF LEADERSHIP

Last, we hear Ratcliffe's thoughts on his own leadership style. In fact, leaders come in many shapes, sizes, and forms. Have you identified your own style? Is it aligned with the needs of the organization and those you're guiding? In growing as a leader, who has influenced you the most? What parts of their style have you adopted, and which features do you choose not to use?

My leadership has always been collaborative. It's my leadership style: to find all the stakeholders, which are all my student athletes, and how they want to do things. Then I give them my opinion of how things should be done. And my hope is that we can come together and find common ground of how things should be done so that we achieve our shared goals. That's been my leadership style all along. The way I've evolved is that probably, sometimes [in the past], I wouldn't be as collaborative as I should have been. I was more: "No. I know better. This is how it should be done, and we're going to do it this way." I've learned over the years to really trust my student athletes more. They have really good ideas, and I know how critical their viewpoint is in mapping out our vision or our goals for the future.

Probably the most important thing I've learned about leadership over the years is that—like I spoke about earlier—we're shaped by the people who have been leaders to us and that we've worked with when we were growing up. But you're not going to be the same leader they are, because you have to stay true to your own personality, who you are, and what your strengths are. You can pick up nuggets from all of them or little ideas, but ultimately you have to figure out what suits you and what your personality is. For example, I couldn't come across as this hard, dictatorial leader. It's not my style, and it's not my personality.

The most important thing I would advise for a leader is to lead by example. You have to be honest, you have to have good sportsmanship, you have to be competitive, you have to be caring, you have to be punctual, you have to do everything. You are a leader to all these people. They're going to look up to you, and they're going to mirror you and your behaviors. You really have to be almost an outstanding citizen in the sense that you need to do things the right way, because they are looking at you. If they see you slipping or doing things the wrong way, it gives them the opportunity to say, "I don't have to do [it right,] either." So, you really have to lead by example. That's the number one piece of advice I'd give someone who wants to be a strong leader.

SUMMARY

This chapter presented the thoughts and opinions of one of the most successful coaches in collegiate sports. Paul Ratcliffe emphasized how his parents and also past coaches impacted his coaching. While he has absorbed aspects of how his influencers got things done, he is also aware that his own personality directs his collaborative approach to leadership. In this culture of excellence, there is a tremendous emphasis on trust and respect, especially respecting others by putting forth your own best effort. In this age of being interconnected with many other people, Ratcliffe's leadership style is primed for success and maximum output, as shown in his unmatched record of continuing excellence and the legacy he will leave of preparing countless young leaders to forge their own path to victory.

CHAPTER 7

LEAD LIKE A ROMAN EMPEROR

It is the responsibility of leadership to work intelligently with what is given and not waste time fantasizing about a world of flawless people and perfect choices.

—MARCUS AURELIUS, *Roman Emperor*

Our story begins with a merchant traveling across vast oceans with a shipload of treasure worth more than its weight in gold. The treasure did not comprise precious stones, money, or spices. It was a product that, back in ancient times, was even more valuable and appealed to the vanity of kings, aristocrats, and wealthy merchants.[1]

Inside Zeno of Citium's cargo hold was Tyrian. At one time, only emperors were allowed to use this precious substance, which was painstakingly harvested by hand from the mucous gland of the murex sea snail. The liquid did not cure any disease, nor did it prevent baldness. Tyrian added no vigor to a person's stride. Rather, it conferred upon its users a sense of vanity in the form of royal purple, which grew brighter and more vibrant with weathering and sunlight. Tyrian is a purple dye.

Thousands of decaying shellfish were cracked open by hundreds of laborers to obtain a few grams of the dye to produce royal or imperial purple for the robes of kings and emperors. A toga with a brilliant strip of Tyrian purple was no small status symbol. Therefore, Zeno, our merchant, was

decidedly worried when storms approached, rocking the ship
and threatening his precious cargo. Unfortunately, disaster
struck, and the ship was battered apart in a furious storm.
By fortune, luck, or just plain chance, Zeno was thrown over-
board and washed up onshore.

From there, Zeno watched as the ship and, more important,
his precious cargo sank to the bottom of the ocean. As one
can imagine, losing not only one's entire fortune, but also a
delivery promised to kings and emperors, was not something
to take lightly. Zeno became despondent. A broken man, he
went searching for meaning in life. At that time, there were
philosophers and oracles who provided guidance. One such
person was the Oracle of Delphi. This priestess said to Zeno,
"Take on the color not of dead shellfish, but of men."

Of course, Zeno had no idea what this meant. He continued on his journey, eventually returning to Athens. Wan-
dering aimlessly, penniless, and despondent, he collapsed in
front of a book stall. He began reading some texts of great
philosophers who were popular at the time. He read a series
about Socrates as well as manuscripts by students of Socrates.
Through these and other writings, he found his answer: the
color of men was in their wisdom, their thoughts, their accu-
mulation of learnings in life. That was what the priestess
had meant.

With this realization, Zeno began his true quest, which,
a decade later, resulted in the founding of his own school.
He said, "My most profitable journey began on the day I was
shipwrecked and lost my entire fortune." Zeno had found
something more valuable than shellfish mucous. Over the
previous ten years, he had learned from the great philosophers of his age that wealth and outward appearances were

small matters. Instead, virtue was the aspiration of great persons. His school, which combined elements of Cynicism and other traditions of Athenian philosophy, laid the foundation for Stoicism.

CAPITAL *STOIC* VS. LOWERCASE *STOIC*

The English language has roots in several languages, including German, Greek, and Latin. Our modern word usage is set in the context of contemporary times. At the end of the day, the meaning of a word comes from how people in a local community use it and understand it. For example, a *lift* in England will mean the elevator. The phrase *what's up?* means "hello" in certain parts of the United States. Words and meanings also change over time.

Accordingly, the words *stoic* and *stoicism* have a layperson's meaning, which may or may not be in line with the meaning and teachings from the capital "S" Stoic school of thought. In modern vernacular, being "stoic" typically means not showing any emotion in the face of adversity. It refers to a personality trait. For example, we might say, "That person is really stoic and never seems happy or sad."

For our purposes, this meaning is inaccurate. The philosophy and practice of "Stoicism" and being a "Stoic" mean many things. Most important, it does not describe someone as unemotional, like Mr. Spock from *Star Trek*. In fact, the Stoic outlook on life includes support for passion, the pursuit of virtues, living in agreement with nature, and exercising reason. The aim is to flourish as human beings.

According to psychotherapist, writer, trainer, and noted Stoicism expert Donald Robertson: "In addition to believing that humans are essentially rational creatures, the Stoics also believed that human nature is inherently social. We have a bond of natural affection toward our children and loved ones, those with whom we identify." Stoics were called "cosmopolitans, or 'citizens of the universe.' Stoic ethics involves cultivating this natural affection toward other people in accord with virtues like justice, fairness, and kindness."[2]

HUMANS ARE FIRST AND FOREMOST THINKING CREATURES

Stoicism makes an important assumption: humans have something that separates us from the inanimate and from the other creatures of the world. There is a quality that makes us unique, says Robertson:

> Stoics argued that humans are first and foremost thinking creatures, capable of exercising reason. Although we share many instincts with animals, it's our ability to think rationally that makes us human. Reason governs our decisions, in a sense—it's our ruling faculty.[3]

Consider that this proposition does not call for the elimination, suppression, or denial of our instincts, emotions, or urges. Rather, it says that we as humans have the ability to make a rational determination of whether such things are good or bad, healthy or unhealthy. According to Robertson:

> The Stoics believed that as we mature in wisdom we increasingly identify with our own capacity for

reasoning, but then we also increasingly identify with others insofar as they're capable of reason. In other words, the wise man extends moral consideration to all rational creatures and views them, in a sense, as his brothers and sisters.[4]

Within the Stoic school of thought, they identified three types of emotion: good, bad, and indifferent, says Robertson:

They have names for many different types of good passion (*eupatheiai*) grouped under three headings: a sense of joy, a healthy aversion to vice, and a healthy desire to help ourselves, and others.

They also believed that we have many irrational desires and emotions like fear, anger, craving, and certain forms of pleasure, which are bad for us or unhealthy. But they also said that our initial automatic feelings are to be viewed as natural and indifferent. These are things like being startled, irritated, blushing, pallor, tensing, shaking, sweating, stammering, and so on. These are our natural reflex reactions before we indulge in them and escalate them into full-blown passions. They're primitive emotional reactions or precursors of emotion, which we share with many animals.[5]

THE LEGACY OF STOIC PHILOSOPHY IN LEADERSHIP

Augustus, the founder of the Roman empire, had Stoic tutors. But probably the most famous Stoic in a leadership position was the Roman emperor Marcus Aurelius, who lived from 121 until 180 CE. Educated by Stoic tutors, he left us an account of his thinking in a set of personal reflections called *Meditations*. Accordingly, Stoicism has a deep and extensive influence in Greek and Roman history. There has been a contemporary re-accounting of these philosophies and texts, with renewed application of Stoicism to many areas of life, touching upon personal development, business interactions, and transformative leadership.

STOICISM IN YOUR LIFE

Today, Stoicism has reemerged as an approach to life. As people have learned more about its teachings and principles, they have realized that it does not advocate an emotionless, rational, Spock-like existence. Its goals are happiness, emotional resilience, and practical techniques to take on the challenges of life in a meaningful way. "Stoic philosophy teaches us not to suppress our unhealthy emotions," says Robertson, "but to transform them into healthy ones by rationally challenging value judgements and other beliefs on which they're based."[6]

CAN YOU LEAD LIKE A ROMAN EMPEROR? AN INTERVIEW WITH DONALD ROBERTSON

Robertson specializes in teaching evidence-based psychological skills. He is known as an expert on the relationship between modern cognitive-behavioral therapy (CBT) and classical Greek and Roman philosophy. He is the author of the 2019 book *How to Think Like a Roman Emperor: The Stoic Philosophy of Marcus Aurelius.*

JIM: Let's start off by asking you what you feel were Marcus
Aurelius's main leadership qualities.

DONALD: I have written a little bit about what Marcus says
on leadership and there are a couple of ways we can
approach it.

We can look at what Stoicism in general would say,
but there's also a way of extracting some points from the
Meditations because Marcus was very interested in modeling excellence, which is a Stoic technique.

The person that he modeled the most, without a
shadow of a doubt, was his adoptive father, the emperor
Antoninus Pius, who was his predecessor. Marcus was
chosen to be an emperor by the emperor Hadrian,
and he doesn't seem to have thought very highly of
Hadrian. And you know, even Hadrian's example seems
to kind of put Marcus off becoming a leader, becoming
an emperor.

But then there was a guy that came in between them,
because Marcus was too young to become emperor. So,
Antoninus Pius succeeded Hadrian, and Marcus seems to
have looked at him and thought: *This guy is an inspiration
to me. He's showing me how someone can be an emperor
and maintain their integrity.*

He's the opposite of Hadrian in many respects, who
Marcus seems to have thought of as a bad emperor in
some ways. So, he says a lot of specific things that he
modeled from Antoninus Pius. He goes into a surprising
amount of detail, writing a decade after Antoninus Pius
died, still describing, still meditating on the lessons you
can learn from this guy.

I ran off to where I tried to categorize them and say, "In bullet-point form, what are the main things?" I'll just hit you with those and then maybe you will have some thoughts about that.

JIM: Sure.

DONALD: The first is that Antoninus Pius had a cheerful and positive attitude, and he got on well with other people. He was a team player and an easy guy to be around.

Second, Antoninus Pius was very hardworking and conscientious. Unlike Hadrian, who had a bit of a butterfly mind, Antoninus was the sort of guy who would sit down and work on something until it was done. He was very patient, even when doing boring tasks, and that's something Marcus watched him doing and learned from him.

Third, he wasn't into flattery, which is something that emperors really traded in. Antoninus Pius wasn't interested in heaping praise and honor on people just to win their favor, and he was kind of indifferent when people tried to flatter him. So, he wasn't easily sucked in by people who were kissing his backside, as it were. Whereas other emperors were often really into that sort of thing.

And number four, I guess converse of that, is that Marcus talks quite a bit about how Antoninus Pius didn't succumb to criticism very easily. He invited ethical feedback from other people. He welcomed it, but he wasn't upset by it. He always took it on the chin and people felt that they could speak plainly to him.

Now, obviously, with other emperors, you'd be frightened to speak your mind in case you get your head chopped off or were sent into exile or something. But Antoninus Pius never punished people for things like that, and they always felt that they could speak freely around him.

Fifth, and finally, Marcus talked a lot about how Antoninus actually led a very simple life. Again, paradoxically, although he was a Roman emperor, he lived like a civilian.

He dressed plainly when he didn't have to wear his ceremonial robes, and Marcus said that he tried to live as closely to the lifestyle of a private citizen as he could. He got rid of many of the ornaments in the Imperial Palace. He did away with many of the bodyguards. He allowed and even invited people to approach him with questions. He tried to be an ordinary guy as much as he could and not allow his position to go to his head.

Those are the five things that Marcus really dwells on in a lot more detail than I have. And in describing these leadership qualities, he really admires his predecessor.

JIM: That's great. And with that example in mind, how did he build on his mentor's legacy to demonstrate this leadership during his own time as emperor?

DONALD: Well, the funny thing is that when we look at history, we think there's a kind of succession of emperors. You know, you've got Hadrian, you've got Antoninus Pius, you've got Marcus Aurelius, then it goes down to Commodus. But if you look more closely, like most things in life, it's not as clean-cut as that, and in fact there's quite a lot of overlap between them.

Actually, Marcus Aurelius served as a second-in-command to Antoninus for about twenty years. And so, there are quite a lot of similarities in the way that they ruled. Marcus didn't really change that much. You know, his policies, his way of ruling, were very similar to his predecessor. The only thing, the main thing, perhaps, would be that Marcus had to deal with a lot more problems than Antoninus Pius did.

He had to deal with several wars, whereas the preceding reign was very peaceful. Also, he embraced philosophy more wholeheartedly than Antoninus Pius. Marcus thought his adoptive father naturally exemplified many of the virtues of Stoicism, although he wasn't really trained in Stoicism as far as we know, and he wasn't a philosopher per se.

I guess if you were to pick on things that characterize his reign, like his predecessor, Marcus collaborated closely with the Senate. He saw himself as a servant of the people. Contrast this with other Roman emperors who were autocrats, acted like dictators, and treated the Senate as underlings, trivialized them, sidelined them, or bullied them.

Marcus saw himself very much as ruling jointly with the Senate and collaborating with them to quite an extraordinary degree. We're told by one historian, Cassius Dio, that when a civil war broke out, Marcus raised the idea of voluntarily stepping down as emperor and appearing before a Senate hearing in order to answer the charges against him. His authority was being impeached, and he said, "I'd be happy to stand down and appear in front of a Senate hearing and respond to the criticisms being made." This is really quite extraordinary, if you think about it. And not how we normally think about autocratic emperors.

JIM: Oh, wow. Yeah, that's rare humility, and also it sounds like he didn't think he was bigger than Rome, as obviously some of his predecessors and those that followed him did.

DONALD: Yeah. And we have the *Meditations*, which give us an insight into his personal attitudes. They were never meant for publication. Thus, we have this kind of window into his soul where we can see how he thinks about things personally. He's writing to himself. And then we have the histories of his reign that describe his outward actions and they're pretty consistent with the stuff that he's saying in his private notes. The two together give us this rounded picture of Marcus, which shows that he really did think of himself as a servant of the people and of the Senate.

JIM: Absolutely. In general, how do you think that leaders, in any realm today, can improve their outcomes? Can such outcomes be achieved by greater control of their thinking and emotions?

DONALD: There are many different aspects to Stoicism that we can talk about. We can talk about this idea of modeling excellence, but another thing that people talk about, which I think you are touching upon, is whether there is a psychological aspect of coping with adversity and dealing, building emotional resilience to a high state, for a high-pressure position. That is certainly a challenge in leadership positions.

Looking back, Antoninus Pius is known for having a very peaceful reign. As soon as Marcus Aurelius became emperor, the Parthians invaded Armenia and a huge war broke out in the Eastern empire. Then at the end of that war, a plague ravaged the empire, killing 10 percent of the population. We believe it may have been smallpox. It's called the Antonine plague. And because the legions were overseas in the East and just beginning to run down to the garrisons and because they were devastated by plague across the northern frontier, the northern tribes banded together and invaded the empire all the way down into northern Italy.

There was a huge war, which was called "The War of Many Nations," and was one of the biggest that they'd ever faced. As such, Marcus faced one catastrophe after another. Cassius Dio says he was the most unfortunate of emperors, and it was almost as if the gods were saying, "We're going to test this guy's Stoicism. We're going to throw everything at him and see how he copes with that."

Marcus had had no military training whatsoever and was kind of thrown into the position of taking operational commanders, the military. The historians say he donned a military cape and robes and rode out from Rome, crossed the isles to Austria, and took command of the largest army ever assembled on a Roman frontier—140,000 men are under his command, which is almost inconceivable today, to think that he was in that position.

And he had to fall back on Stoicism as a way of coping with the stress. To cap it all, his Stoic mentor, Junius

Rusticus, died around this time, perhaps of the plague. And I believe that's why Marcus started writing his journal.

We could say that, through war and plague, Marcus lost a lot of people that he had turned to as mentors. He was kind of isolated. He left Rome for the first time. He sat down and started writing, which we believe was originally not called the *Meditations*. Incidentally, the earliest manuscript we've got is titled *To Himself*, and the *Meditations* is almost like a letter or a series of notes that he's writing to himself as if he's becoming his own teacher, his own mentor in Stoicism.

He does this as he is rising to the position of taking responsibility for managing himself, doing therapy on himself. Marcus actually refers to Rusticus, who had just died, as a therapist,. And so now Marcus is figuring out a way to take over that role and work on his own emotions through writing.

JIM: The start of *Meditations* offers a great exercise for all leaders and for all of us in terms of who are the people that have influenced us the most, asking us to reflect on what their values are and how we can better emulate our role models.

DONALD: Yes, there is a whole chapter dedicated to that exercise. I think there are, if I remember right, about sixteen different people that he makes a summary of the qualities that he wants to model from them, and some of them aren't particularly good people. One of them is his co-emperor and his adopted brother, Lucius Verus, who by all accounts was a terrible emperor, an alcoholic, and probably a gambling addict. He didn't perform well as emperor, and Marcus, in a way, damns him with faint praise, but he still finds something admirable in the guy. He says he was loyal and affectionate, like it was damning with faint praise—the guy is an emperor. But that's all he can say about him. But nevertheless, he finds something worth learning and emulating from Verus.

JIM: Yeah, I think it shows how loyal Marcus was and affectionate to his brother, who maybe didn't deserve it.

DONALD: You know, people have this misconception that Stoicism is unemotional. It's like being like Mr. Spock or being like a robot, or something like that, or being cold, and that's not at all true. Marcus actually says in that chapter that the qualities of a great Stoic ought to be full of love. The Greek word is *philastorge*, which is a little tricky to translate, but it's that kind of paternal love or soft brotherly love. It's being full of love and yet free from kind of pathological or unhealthy passions.

And he's not saying that we should be unemotional, quite the contrary. He's saying we should replace unhealthy emotions with healthy ones. And again, what he's saying there is, "What can I model from my adopted brother?" Two of the main things are his loyalty and his affection. And we have a cache of Marcus Aurelius's private letters to his rhetoric tutor Fronto that were discovered in the middle of the nineteenth century. The thing that really jumps out about those letters is just how incredibly affectionate that he was as a father and toward his friends.

I think to be a Stoic means to be a very warm and friendly, a kind of very genial person.

JIM: Absolutely. And can you talk to us a little bit more about how he practiced humility? You touched on it earlier, saying he did away with this huge number of bodyguards and dressed more modestly than other emperors had, and this type of thing. What were some other ways that he practiced humility, which again might be the complete opposite that most people might think, given the example of some of his fellow emperors?

DONALD: There are a whole bunch of things that he did. One of the first things is that for the very first time in Roman history, Marcus appointed a co-emperor. When he was appointed emperor, he immediately insisted that they input the Senate, appointing his adoptive brother Lucius Verus to rule jointly with them. He believed that the rule of an emperor should be shared not only with the Senate, but also with an albeit-somewhat-junior co-emperor. It also seems that throughout his reign he was planning to do that with Commodus, his own successor, although for a number of reasons it didn't work out.

So that's the first thing. That's a very unusual step that in some way waters down the possession of emperor from the role of an autocrat to more of a presidential role almost. And he said that on all major decisions and all major appointments, he made the point of consulting with the Senate to get their approval beforehand. He also often dressed as a philosopher. He would just dress in plain robes. We see this in the *Meditations*, and we're told in the histories, although it seems kind of extraordinary, but it's often the case that we get little fragments of archaeological evidence. There's a statuette of Marcus that was found in Egypt that shows him wearing civilian dress, a kind of Greek shocker. And apparently, it seems that when he was in Egypt, he went around dressed as an ordinary citizen, which would have been completely the opposite of an emperor like Hadrian.

Another little nugget about Marcus is that, at the beginning of the Marcomannic Wars, we're told that the Roman treasury was depleted, and they were struggling to raise funds for the war. Marcus held an auction at the Forum in Rome where he sold off his wife's dresses, gems that Hadrian had hoarded, statues, and a whole lot of items from his Imperial Palace. He sold them all off, which would be like the Queen of England having an auction to sell off the crown jewels to fund the military during a crisis.

JIM: You mentioned that basically Marcus was thrust into a position of having to be commander in chief with no military experience. He then takes command of this army. What does he have to say about this experience and how it formed and shaped him as a person, even more so than as a kind of de facto general?

DONALD: It's really curious, because in the *Meditations* many scholars comment on this. It's odd because he doesn't explicitly say much about what's going on around him. On the other hand, he does make many references to everyday things, like he'll talk about the river. He'll talk about the sparrows and other birds. He'll talk in abstract terms of people that are meddling or treacherous, but he never actually uses the phrase *Marcomannic Wars* anywhere in the book. He mentions one of his enemies once very briefly in passing, and then there's one very graphic passage where [he] mentions seeing several heads and limbs on a battlefield, but he turns this into a metaphor for being alienated emotionally from the rest of mankind. He said that when you view someone as your enemy, there's something unnatural about that.

You alienate yourself from your brother, and it is eerie and unnatural seeing a head lying several feet away from a body on the battlefield. He has this weird tendency to take things that he sees in everyday life and turn them into metaphors for philosophy. There are many references to things around him, but not specific historical references, which is really quite surprising because he's literally writing this on the front line of the Marcomannic Wars. And in the middle of a military camp, it's really quite bizarre in a way, but we can kind of read between the lines perhaps and see some of the ways that it may have shaped his character. For example, in the passage that opens book two, which is perhaps the most famous passage in the *Mediations,* he says, . . . [in effect,] every morning when you wake up, tell yourself that you're going to meet people who are treacherous, meddling, and deceptive and just learn to accept these things and not to be shocked by them.

Interestingly, when you read the *Meditations*, because of this lack of reference to historical details, sometimes it seems like he's just talking generally about some petty relationship pressures, and he may be, but he was also faced with world historic betrayals on a huge scale. Actually, the whole war that he was fighting was triggered by a Marcomannic king called Ballomar, who had been conspiring for years against him and had broken a peace treaty. Therefore, maybe when he says, [in effect,] every day, tell yourself you're going to be faced with betrayals, he's talking about this huge historic event, which may have been one of the things on his mind. As such, he's training himself to be completely unfazed by these things.

JIM: What other personalities and flaws does he admit to struggling with, and how did he use Stoic principles to address them?

DONALD: Well, I should say, we can see a kind of progression. If we look at the story, there are hints that over the years there were times when he struggled with anger and then kind of learned to conquer it. Toward the end of his life, there was a civil war, and a guy that was one of his senior generals, his most senior general in the East, declared himself emperor. So, for a short period of time, about three months, there was a rival emperor. Then Avidius Cassius dies, and something really extraordinary happens. We have this amazing, bizarre speech that Marcus delivers to his legion, and he does something, which I find utterly shocking and which I think the Romans were absolutely

LEAD LIKE A ROMAN EMPEROR 151

amazed by: he gives a speech to the legion saying that he's going to pardon the guys that conspired against him and, in fact, everybody involved in the civil war.

It seems like a remarkable thing to stand and announce to an army that's about to march against these guys [in effect]: "We're going to march across the empire to put down the civil war, but before we do that, I'm officially declaring that I'm pardoning everybody involved in it. We're going to have to fight them anyway, but I'm not going to persecute anybody that's involved in this. There are not going to be any repercussions for them."

This in turn led to the end of the war because Avidius Cassius's officers maybe had some initial defeats, and they decided that it wasn't worth fighting anymore, because they were all going to be pardoned anyway. Therefore, the only person that wants to continue the fight was Avidius Cassius. Well, his officers assassinated him and put his head in a bag and delivered it to Marcus. And then he said he wished he had an opportunity to pardon Cassius as well.

He was good to his word. He pardoned everybody involved. He said, let's treat it as water under the bridge and try and move on and rebuild things. He even protected Avidius Cassius's family from persecution. This was so extraordinary. But after Marcus died, one of the first things that his son Commodus did was to reverse all that he had done, and the conspirators were hunted down and burned alive as traitors. Obviously, Commodus felt very uncomfortable with Marcus's leniency.

JIM: That's quite remarkable. Magnanimity, really.

DONALD: And it could backfire. But in this case, it actually worked in his favor and ended the civil war with minimal bloodshed.

I suppose one of the other things that may be worth mentioning about Marcus as a leader is that definitely part of the narrative of his life is that, when he went to the northern frontier, he was generally perceived as an inappropriate commander in chief because he didn't have military experience. Hence, Avidius Cassius and other people apparently called him a philosophical old woman. They didn't really think that he was up to the task, and people probably had thought [he] was a real fish out of water, taking command of the legions. Well, a few years later, by the end of the first Marcomannic War, there are multiple pieces of evidence to suggest that this thinking had been transformed and the legions absolutely idolized him now as a commander in chief and they saw him as an accomplished military commander and were steadfastly loyal to him.

One of the characteristics of the civil war [included] several legions based in what's now Russia and Turkey who were basically isolated and surrounded by the rebel army. The idea was that they would flip and go over to the other side, but they didn't. They stood their ground, to everyone's surprise. And that's an indication of the way that Marcus had won loyalty, at least from some of the legions that were most familiar with him.

Avidius Cassius, his rival, was the opposite kind of leader. He was known for being extremely strict. In the Roman army, that meant, for example, flogging people on a regular basis, punishing his troops, and decimating them if there was any sign of disloyalty. There's even a story that Avidius Cassius sought to frighten the enemy into submission by having dozens of them tied to a huge wooden pole in a hole and setting it on fire so that the villagers from miles around could see their countrymen burning alive. Cassius's policy or style as a military commander was to terrorize the enemy so that they wouldn't dare defy the Romans. Meanwhile, Marcus saw that this was a very short-term solution and it was bound to backfire and create more enemies in the long run. He was much more interested in diplomacy, a kind of dovish approach, and negotiating peace for the long term.

I guess another thing I should throw in, to tie it more to Stoicism and the *Meditations,* is another oddity that ties in with the philosophy. Marcus never really talks about Roman citizens in the *Meditations*, but he talks a lot, on almost every page, about social virtue, cosmopolitanism, natural affection, the virtue of justice, fairness, beneficence, and generosity. As such, he's talking about how to interact with society in general, but he hardly ever mentioned Roman citizens. He always talks about other human beings, and it seems clear that even at one point he mentions the enemy, the Sarmations, that he views them as his brothers because he's a Stoic and is cosmopolitan. Therefore, on one level he has this obligation to represent the citizens of the Roman empire, but he doesn't want to view the barbarians, as it were, as the enemies, as being like aliens to him.

He sees them as his brothers, as his kin. He's resisting the idea of getting angry with them and viewing them as the bad guys. They're just other human beings that he happens to be in conflict with. And he also knows that at certain points they might become his allies and often he is attempting to negotiate peace with them. Marcus was a highly accomplished communicator, I would say. And we can see that in his private life. There's one thing that really stands out as evidence of the way he talks to people in his letters of this tremendous ability that he has to resolve arguments even between his personal friends. He was clearly a highly skilled diplomat.

JIM: Progressing to Stoicism in general, and again thinking about this, the concept of leadership, when a leader is trying to take their team or organization through a seemingly insurmountable challenge, what might be a Stoic principle or two that could help the leader both lead themselves better and also the people that are depending on them for leadership?

DONALD: This is a good opportunity to get back to some Stoic basics and some of the more popular principles of Stoicism today. First, we have a Stoic author, in fact the author, the philosopher that Marcus really has mentioned most often is Epictetus, who is the most famous Stoic teacher of Rome, and in the entire history of the Roman republic or the empire. Epictetus left us transcripts of his discourses about teaching his philosophy students. We also have this little book called the *Enchiridion*, a handbook, which is literally a bunch of guidelines, a summary of how to live like a Stoic written by one of his students called Arrian, who was actually a Roman general. In the

first sentence of the *Enchiridion*, we've got a really simplified guide to the psychology of Stoicism. The opening
sentence of it quite famously says, *some things are up to
us and other things are not.*

That's a truism, right? Some people might read that
and think you are kind of stating the obvious. And what
is the point in saying some things are up to us and other
things are not—that's just glaringly obvious, isn't it?
But the Stoics were smart enough to realize that even
though that's self-evidently true, people constantly act
as if they've forgotten it. And as if they're quite confused about this boundary between what's up to them
and what's not, as people behave and emote constantly
about things that aren't under their direct control, or
they take too much responsibility for things that they
can't control and struggle against them emotionally. The
flip side of this is that people consistently neglect to take
responsibility for things that actually are under their
voluntary control.

This distinction actually is the basis of a very famous
saying that was popularized by Alcoholics Anonymous
called the serenity prayer, which you're probably also
familiar with. It says, "God, give me the serenity to accept
the things I cannot change, the courage to change the
things I can, and the wisdom to know the difference." And
that perfectly encapsulates this opening sentence of the
Enchiridion. The basic principles of Stoicism, the wisdom
of Stoicism, consists in knowing the difference between
the things that we can control and the things that we
can't, and this is very good psychology. It's very astute.

I won't go into a lot of detail about this, but even in working with clients with anxiety disorders today, there are a number of quite specific technical reasons that by making that distinction can be of quite fundamental importance to the treatment. We can definitely see that people who suffer from pathological anxiety have a tendency to get confused about where this line is drawn between the things that they control and the things that they can't.

JIM: Focus on the process, don't worry about the result.

DONALD: The Stoics have an entire philosophy of life that is based around this idea of focusing on the process. They called this process *arete*, or virtue. That's what they mean. *Arete* is the way that you do stuff. It's the quality of your action in the present moment. *Arete* is a process. It's translated as virtue, but that's a bad translation. It would be better to translate it more broadly as just kind of doing your best, or excellence of character, as the scholars often say.

JIM: I love the view-from-a-mountaintop idea. I think that's great for leaders in terms of being able to detach from their situation and to look more objectively at what might be the best next step. Can you tell us briefly about that?

DONALD: We call this the view from above. We don't know what most of these techniques were called by the Stoics, but this name is given to it by a French scholar called Pierre Hadot, who is an expert on Hellenistic

philosophy. He called it the view from above. And that's
what most people call it today. Marcus talks about it
repeatedly, especially toward the end of the *Meditations*. I'll mention two things about it. One is Athens,
the birthplace of Stoicism, is surrounded by hills. And
in the middle of Athens, there's a big hole that grew
around a hill that had accessibility on top originally, like
many ancient cities and towns. And that's the Acropolis
of Athens. It became a sacred place; there was a temple
to Athena there. Socrates and other Greek philosophers
would go up the Acropolis and the view that they would
have from there would be the Agora, the marketplace
where there were public assemblies, traders, and people
debating philosophy.

This is the view from above that Marcus Aurelius
describes; he even uses the word *Agora*. Well, it's literally
the view that Athenians would be familiar with looking
down from the sacred hill in the middle of the city. If
you're a tourist today, you can go there for a day and look
down and you'll literally get the view from above. You
could also say the view from the Gods, the view of Zeus
looking down from Mount Olympus.

I'll relate this to something in modern cognitive
therapy, which I want to mention because many people
could benefit from it today very easily. For example, when
someone comes into therapy and they say they're worrying about losing their job or their girlfriend dumping
them or some catastrophe, the cognitive therapist's easiest
technique arguably is to say, well, suppose your girlfriend
does dump you, what would probably happen next?

And then the patient expands their perspective chronologically by doing that. They'll say, I guess I'll be really depressed, and I'll stay at home and just watch Netflix or whatever. And then the cognitive therapist will say, well then, what will probably happen next? And they'll say, well, I guess eventually, you know, maybe go out and hang out with some of my friends or something like that. And then probably what will happen next? Well, I guess eventually I'll meet somebody or date them or whatever. Then what will probably happen next? Well, I guess I'll probably get in another relationship and I'll start to move on.

And you can see that in just about any field: catastrophe. It's interesting that when you expand the chronological perspective, in almost any field, catastrophe seems less overwhelming. And the Stoics knew that two-and-a-half thousand years ago. Thus, they systematically trained themselves in a whole variety of different ways to expand both the chronological and the spatial perspective. Sometimes they deleted these two things independently. Sometimes they would do it both at the same time.

JIM: Yeah. Can you discuss this in regard to how this technique could help people to improve their pain management where the pain is in a particular location in space and then also it's temporary?

DONALD: Yeah. This often helps people when they're suffering from pain as well, actually as a way of coping. For example, Marcus would tell himself when he was suffering with pain or discomfort to focus on the fact that he only needs to deal with the present moment. And that in itself shouldn't seem overwhelming to him because it's just a moment that I need to deal with. And then the next moment and then the next moment, kind of one step at a time. Nothing lasts forever. Even pain waxes and wanes; it gets better and it gets worse. Thus, both focusing on the present and also focusing on that broader perspective seems to definitely help people. I won't go into details on why, but just one little aside—in modern psychology, we know that when people experience pathological emotions, there's a narrowing of the scope of their attention cognitively.

When people are anxious, they do this thing called threat monitoring, which is like a laser beam. They become really focused on any negative or threatening aspects of the situation and that's like putting things under a magnifying glass that intensifies your emotional reaction. If you broaden your perspective, that inherently counteracts the way that your brain tends to work when it's anxious. It puts you in an opposing frame of mind and one in which multiple stimuli are now entering your mind, so you have a more complex and a more moderate emotional response than you would if you just put a magnifying glass onto the worst part of the situation. The Stoics were really smart. They figured this out a really long time ago.

Edited for brevity and clarity.

LEADERSHIP REFLECTIONS

- What phrases or principles have you developed to practice and strengthen your ability to deal with daily problems, issues, or challenges?

- A commonly held principle in elite sports, meditation practices, and Stoicism is to focus on the process. How do you encourage this in your leadership role?

- What have you done in past experiences that was an atypical response to a challenge?

- When facing a crisis or overwhelming situation, how have you broadened the perspective to better deal with a situation?

SUMMARY

In this chapter, we learned about several key principles from Stoic philosophy. First and foremost, one should have a goal in life. Instead of just going through the motions or tackling all of life's daily problems one day, one problem at a time, there should be a larger goal. Next, to constantly move toward this goal, there are several Stoic strategies. Some of them can also be thought of as psychological strategies, such as reframing a negative situation into a challenge; acknowledging an insult, but choosing to ignore it; noting some anger, anxiety, or envy, but not acting on it; negative visualization; and dichotomy of control. Other strategies include refocusing to a broader perspective, looking down from atop the hill as they say, or focusing on the process—the task presently at hand.

Putting these strategies into practice requires use and repetition, like training for a sport. If you are always using hacks and shortcuts and giving yourself the easy way out, then you'll get little practice and no challenging workouts. And unless you're particularly lucky, the inevitable big challenge will come along. As a Stoic, you'll have been in constant training, and you'll be able to flex your mental muscles and rise to the occasion.

CHAPTER 8

THE LEADER'S MISSION

We all have a responsibility to try and make this world better,
whether it's through our work, the causes we champion, the way
that we treat people, or the values we impart to the next generation.

—DANIEL LUBETZKY, *Philanthropist, Author,*
and Founder and Executive Chairman of KIND LLC

When you think about the glamorous life of a billionaire social entrepreneur, is this the image that comes to mind? "I'd walk down Broadway starting at seven in the morning, carrying a fake leather case. I'd taken out my legal briefs and filled it up with jars of sun-dried tomato spread and pieces of bread. I would go store by store to let people try the product, and then I would finish at 7:00 p.m. Once I had enough orders and entered them in my computer, I'd then go and deliver the product. I had a beat-up Cougar, and I had to fill it up with boxes and close the trunk with duct tape. When I was going to a delivery, I'd take the duct tape off, get the boxes out, deliver them, and come back before I got a ticket."[1]

For the first few years of his business career, this was reality for KIND founder Daniel Lubetzky. As arduous as his daily grind was, however, it pales in comparison to what his father experienced in the Nazi concentration camp Dachau, fifty years earlier.

FROM THE END, A NEW BEGINNING

Roman Lubetzky stood shivering as the biting wind blew down from northern Germany into the concentration camp in Upper Bavaria that he was now expected to think of as "home." But for anyone, let alone this gaunt, hollow-cheeked teenager, there was nothing comforting or home-like about the oppressive surroundings he now found himself in: fences topped with razor wire, towers manned by machine-gun-toting guards, barren barracks with lice-infested beds and frost-coated walls.

And then there were the fires that burned all day and night, the chimneys belching foul-smelling smoke and ash into the sky. The friends who disappeared seemingly without a trace. The mother he hadn't seen since they were herded into separate trucks by gruff Nazi soldiers in Lithuania's Kovno Ghetto. Some days, it seemed to Roman that he had nothing to live for. On other days, he seemed sure to die, none less so than on April 28, 1945, when his captors led Roman, his brother Larry, and their father on a death march into the mountains, where their guards intended to push them down an impossibly steep slope.

Escape seemed hopeless, but as the rising sun bathed the hillside in warm light the next morning, Roman awoke to find that the German soldiers had fled. He joined his father and their fellow survivors in staggering to a nearby village. Later that day, the tanks of the advancing 522nd Field Artillery Battalion rolled in and saved the emaciated prisoners from their Nazi nightmare. That same day, the US Seventh Army's 45th Infantry Division and US 42nd

Rainbow Division liberated another thirty thousand Holocaust survivors from Dachau and its subcamp. Fifteen-year-
old Roman would never stop having nightmares. But he was
finally free.[2]

Once he had recovered physically from imprisonment
in Nazi Germany's first concentration camp, Roman immi-
grated to Mexico to start a new life with his father. Due first
to the pogroms and then to imprisonment in the living hell
of Dachau, Roman's schooling had been abruptly halted in
the third grade. But ever the self-starter, he didn't let a lack
of formal education hold him back, teaching himself to read,
devouring encyclopedias cover to cover, and allowing curios-
ity to guide his learning wherever it wandered.[3]

What he may have lacked in test scores or grades, Roman
more than made up for with sheer gumption. As a young
man, he set up a successful duty-free company. He also found
in himself a flair for business rooted in his conversational
skills, commitment to treating suppliers and customers fairly,
and innate kindness. "For him, life could have ended after
the Holocaust, but he chose to let it begin. He approached
every day with optimism, every job with devotion and every
stranger with compassion," his son told CNN. "He treated
everyone as an equal, whether it was the bank teller or the
bank president."[4]

LEADERSHIP REFLECTIONS

- How can you rise above your circumstances to reach for higher goals?

- Do you resent the daily grind or embrace it as a necessary step on your journey?

- Think of an experience you've always viewed as negative, and then try to find a positive takeaway.

A LIGHT IN THE DARKNESS

Some of Daniel Lubetzky's earliest childhood memories are of the stories his father told him about his grueling wartime experiences. Though his mother, Sonia, thought her son was too young for such tales, Roman knew that he could impart more wisdom to his son through them than he'd find in any book or classroom. While he had suffered at the hands of the Nazis and witnessed terrible things no child should ever see, Roman recounted the story of how, as he leaned against the Dachau perimeter fence, weak with hunger, a German guard threw half a potato at his feet. Though it might seem insignificant, this gesture could have led to the soldier being court-martialed or put in front of a firing squad. Perhaps the act didn't atone for whatever cruelties the guard may have inflicted on other prisoners, but it saved a starving boy's life and inspired his heart. "It was important to my father to pass along how dark humanity can be, and how, in the midst of that darkness, you can bring light," Lubetzky later told an interviewer.[5]

Such storytelling inspired the young man to continue his father's legacy and live out the principles of kindness, decency, and concern for others every single day. His dad didn't merely talk about living by the Golden Rule: he demonstrated it again and again. After Roman passed away in 2003, Lubetzky told an interviewer how he remembered seeing his father sharing generously with the homeless. "My father regularly gave money to a blind man he saw begging on the street. Once, he noticed that the beggar got into a fancy car and drove away. When he told me this story, I asked him if he was upset to be the victim of a con artist. He said, 'I'd rather make the mistake of giving to someone who doesn't need it than run the risk of not giving to someone who does.'"[6]

His dad's generosity made an indelible imprint on young Lubetzky's heart, while his principle-driven business ventures kindled an entrepreneurial spark that burst into flame while he was still in grade school. In his book *Do the KIND Thing*, Lubetzky reveals that he started his first business when he was six or seven, staging a carnival for his cousins and three siblings and charging them a few pesos to play a ring toss game, giving a spicy Mexican candy called *chamoy* or a stick of chewing gum as prizes. Soon, he progressed to hosting magic shows for family and friends and was so charismatic that he began to get paid bookings from neighborhood families.

Performing as "The Great HouDani" alongside his friends Jaime (masquerading as "The Great HouJaime) and Gregorio (the clown Eggoletto), Lubetzky performed at bar mitzvahs, birthday parties, and schools. Their best gig was at a department store partly owned by Jaime's parents. Their performance on El Día de los Niños (Children's Day) netted the wide-eyed boys the equivalent of eighty dollars. Demonstrating that they weren't just in it for the money, the precocious trio also put on free shows at retirement homes, the local children's hospital, and a center for kids with developmental delays.[7]

LEADERSHIP REFLECTIONS

· How are you encouraging your children or younger relatives to thrive?

· Do you give generously?

· What lessons did your parents or grandparents share and how can you apply what they taught you?

CUT FROM A DIFFERENT CLOTH

At age twelve, Lubetzky decided that, while he enjoyed the allure of the magic show stage, he wanted to learn more about how real businesses operated. So, he convinced his parents to let him work in a textile factory over summer break, despite the company being located in one of the roughest parts of Mexico City. "It wasn't very easy to discourage you from anything," Lubetzky's mother told him when he was writing his book. "When you set your mind to something, you did it."[8] His daily duties weren't easy: hoisting heavy rolls of cloth on one of his bony shoulders and carrying them to multiple delivery locations as the triple-digit heat sucked the air from his lungs and perspiration soaked his shirt.

Shortly after finishing his first proper summer job, Lubetzky's parents moved him and his three siblings to San Antonio, Texas, where his dad continued expanding his duty-free operation. Seeing that kiosks at the flea market did brisk business and enjoying listening to the banter as traders haggled with their customers, Lubetzky came up with the idea of setting up his own stall. His dad introduced him to several suppliers, who agreed to sell the bold sixteen-year-old watches at wholesale prices.

Eventually, he began buying higher-end watches and clocks from Citizen at overstock liquidations, and did a roaring trade with his twelve-year-old brother, Sioma, acting as his assistant. By Lubetzky's freshman year of college, he and his brother had upgraded their operation and rented booths at Ingram Park Mall and the ritzy North Star Mall. Realizing there were only so many classes they could skip before their grades began slipping, Lubetzky soon hired a cadre of fellow students to fill in when they had class.[9]

During his junior year at Trinity University, Lubetzky left his burgeoning business in his brother's capable hands while he did a study-abroad program in France and Israel. He was so captivated by the subject of Israeli-Arab relations that he decided to focus his senior thesis on it. Toiling late into the night and every weekend, Lubetzky had soon expanded his argument to 268 pages.

"The theory that I conceived while I was here at Trinity is that, as people interact with one another in the business world, under the right conditions, it can shatter cultural stereotypes," Lubetzky told a packed auditorium at his alma mater in March 2019. "And it can help people humanize one another."[10]

LEADERSHIP REFLECTIONS

· How could you benefit from learning about another profession?

· What tasks should you keep doing yourself, and which could you delegate to others?

· Who in your network can help take your career to the next level? And how can you help them do likewise?

YOU DO WHAT I COULDN'T

After graduating from Trinity, Lubetzky applied to several law schools and eagerly accepted an offer from Stanford. Though soon afterward, he began to have doubts and asked his father if he could join him in his duty-free business instead. Roman liked the idea of working side by side with his son, but challenged Daniel to take advantage of an opportunity he'd never been given. "He himself had dreamed of becoming a doctor, but his education had come to an end when the Germans invaded Lithuania," Lubetzky wrote in his book. "It was a testament to his selflessness that he wanted me to aim higher." So, after a series of long conversations, Lubetzky decided to heed his dad's advice and headed to California.[11]

At Stanford, he was fortunate enough to study under some of the world's most talented law professors. Lubetzky recalls one in particular who helped him progress his ideas for bringing peace to the Middle East through business. Professor Emeritus Byron Sher, who would later serve in the California State Assembly and Senate, tasked his class with writing a piece of legislation. Lubetzky chose to focus his bill on ways that Congress could create joint Israeli-Palestinian ventures. The paper was so well executed that Sher encouraged Lubetzky to send it to legal publications. Eventually it made its way into the *Michigan Journal of International Law*—no mean feat for a student who had yet to pass the bar exam.

That came around soon enough, and Lubetzky passed, also earning his law degree from Stanford. The law firm he had interned at, Sullivan & Cromwell (S&C), saw his potential and offered him a full-time position. He had a second offer from McKinsey & Company's Mexico City office. So now, Lubetzky found himself at another crossroads. Would he choose to continue in the legal profession with S&C, or take a diversion into the consulting world with McKinsey?

President Bill Clinton complicated matters by introducing a third path. As Lubetzky sat around with some friends, the forty-second president appeared on TV, hosting PLO leader Yasser Arafat and Israeli prime minister Yitzhak Rabin in the White House Rose Garden to celebrate the Oslo Accords that led to a temporary cease-fire. "I had dreamed about peace in the region since my childhood," Lubetzky later recalled. "I needed to support these nascent peace efforts."[12]

With this in mind, Lubetzky applied for the Haas/Koshland Memorial Award, which provided him with a $10,000 grant to support him during a year in Israel. But this came at a cost, as he had to turn down the McKinsey offer and take a leave of absence from S&C. After consulting his parents and mentors, Lubetzky realized that he had no choice but to pursue his true calling, even though it meant trading the security of a six-figure income with a prestigious firm for uncertainty.

LEADERSHIP REFLECTIONS

· What's a new possibility for your career or life you'd like to explore?

· When was the last time you stepped outside your comfort zone?

· Who can you consult to encourage you to pursue both passion and purpose?

THE LAST JAR

The next thing he knew, Lubetzky was in Tel Aviv signing a lease on a small apartment. Once he settled in, he began researching business in the country and identified several areas that showed the greatest promise for building bridges across sectarian lines, including food processing, cosmetics, and apparel. Soon he realized that his idea of starting a consultancy wasn't going to fly. If he was going to further his mission, Lubetzky would have to get his hands dirty. As fate would have it, there was a savory solution to the dilemma of what he should do next. Taking a much-needed break from his research, Lubetzky wandered down the street to a corner store. Perusing the shelves filled with unfamiliar local fare, his eyes settled on a jar of bright red paste. He picked it up, read the label, and saw that it was sun-dried tomato spread.

Wondering what it would taste like (back in 1994, sun-dried tomatoes weren't as common as they are now), Lubetzky bought it and headed home.

Spreading a generous dollop on pita bread and popping a piece into his mouth, he experienced a flavor explosion. Soon he'd eaten the whole thing. Heading back to the store the next morning, Lubetzky was disappointed to learn that not only had he bought the last jar, but the company had gone bankrupt. In this most unlikely setting, an epiphany washed over him like an ocean wave. What if he could resurrect this business, source the ingredients from different Middle East nations, and bring people together in doing so?

Going into full detective mode, Lubetzky got the name of the distributor from the store owner, which led him to the manufacturer, Yoel Benesh. After getting past the man's initial skepticism—after all, the idea of a veteran businessman trusting a kid from another country to bring his company back to life sounded crazy even to Lubetzky—the two met at the factory. Here, Lubetzky was surprised to see that instead of relying on an automated assembly line, Yoel's workforce had been mixing each batch by hand.[13] In addition to this time-consuming process that drove up production costs, Lubetzky soon discovered other inefficiencies. Benesh was paying too much for glass jars from Portugal and premium olive oil and sun-dried tomatoes from Italy. He'd also failed to make a mark in the tough US market, while struggling to compete against well-established Italian and Greek brands in Europe.

Though Benesh was initially unsure how "a lawyer with no experience in the food business" could help him, he warmed to the young man. And once he heard Lubetzky's vision of cross-cultural cooperation, he bought in immediately.[14] So, Lubetzky got to work doing what he'd always done best: fostering relationships and solving problems. He soon found a cheaper glass jar maker in Egypt, a tomato grower in Turkey, and Palestinian and Israeli villagers who produced olive oil and basil.

While recognizing that solving a company's supply chain challenges couldn't overcome the long-standing geopolitical issues in the region, Lubetzky was convinced that he and new partners like Benesh could at least do something positive among the various ethnic groups they were teaming up with. "As they trade with one another, they hopefully are shattering cultural stereotypes and discovering each other's humanity, and then they're gaining a vested interest in preserving those relationships because they're making money together," Lubetzky said in an interview.[15]

LEADERSHIP REFLECTIONS

- When you're faced with a high-risk, high-reward opportunity, will you take it? If not, what's holding you back?

- How can you use your resources to bring people from different backgrounds together?

- What's an opportunity for your business to make a difference in your community?

LIFE OF A SALESMAN

Once the production pipeline was secure, Lubetzky decided he could best serve his new company, which he called

PeaceWorks, by making connections and working retail channels back in the United States. Renting the cheapest apartment he could find in Manhattan, he discovered that the landlord had a basement storeroom that he would let Lubetzky use to stash jars of his sun-dried tomato spread (now branded as Moshe and Ali's) and a line of Dead Sea salt-based cosmetics. The only catch? There were no windows, and he'd have to share space with a line of laundry machines used at all hours by his fellow tenants.

Lubetzky's days soon settled into a familiar, if demanding, rhythm. He'd wake before dawn, load up his briefcase with samples, go down a list of every food store in Manhattan, and, eventually, the entire city of New York. Whenever the seemingly endless stream of noes got to him, or he wondered if he would have been better off in a cushy law office than traipsing all over town like a real-life Willy Loman, Lubetzky reflected on his driving purpose. "The people [in Israel and Palestine] deserved to live in peace. I also thought about my father, and what he went through as a child during the Second World War and as a kid in a concentration camp. That put my problems in perspective and reminded me of my mission."[16]

As he struggled to get PeaceWorks off the ground, Lubetzky was further discouraged when he saw news reports of bombings and missile attacks in the very region he was trying to reconcile. Day after day, videos showed burned-out buildings, broken bodies on stretchers, and crying children looking desperately for their parents. "I wondered if it was a modern mirage, if what I was doing could really make a difference," he told a student reporter at Stanford. When Lubetzky shared his concerns with his suppliers in Israel,

Palestine, and Egypt, they urged him to keep going. "They said, 'This is our livelihood; this is our future. You can't just walk away. We need to raise our voices even louder and stand up against extremism even more.' It was an interesting wake-up call for me—and made me realize that people's lives depended on this. It wasn't just a paper for a class. I needed to be steadfast and serious."[17]

So Lubetzky buckled down and redoubled his efforts to get PeaceWorks products into as many stores as possible. When money was tight, as it usually was, he'd go to a cheap, all-you-can-eat buffet for a single daily meal. Yet while he was the one carrying a heavy, fit-to-burst briefcase through the snowy streets of Manhattan day after day, Lubetzky didn't have to go it alone. Who were the first two investors in PeaceWorks? None other than his best friends from child-hood, Jaime and Gregorio, with whom he'd performed magic shows while growing up in Mexico City.[18]

After several years of hard work, Lubetzky finally achieved a breakthrough, persuading a manager at Zabar's—one of New York's go-to destinations for gourmands—to let him do an in-store demo. It went well. He sold a couple of cases and was invited back. Soon, Fairway Market, West-side Market, and other shops offered him similar oppor-tunities. Before long, PeaceWorks products were available in more than two hundred locations across the city. Begin-ning to think bigger, he also scored a deal with Haddon House, a major distributor located between New York and Philadelphia.[19] At last, Lubetzky was being rewarded for his bold decision to forgo a legal career in favor of social entrepreneurship.

LEADERSHIP REFLECTIONS

- What are you going to do to work both smarter and harder?

- Which perceived failures can you turn into lessons?

- When you're struggling, what's the mission you can use to remotivate yourself and your team?

DOING THE KIND THING

His first multinational, mission-driven business was born from a fortuitous, hunger-driven trip to the grocery store, but Lubetzky's next venture would be birthed by hardship. Just as it seemed that PeaceWorks was riding high, its only million-dollar client canceled its contract, plunging the company back into the red. The next loss in his life would take an even greater toll, when Roman Lubetzky passed away in January 2003.[20] Searching for solace in the wake of his dad's death, Lubetzky continued to travel all over the United States trying to find a replacement for his biggest buyer. As his mind jumped between his favorite memories of his father and ideas for helping his business bounce back, Lubetzky realized that he was under-provisioned for his relentless travels. Sure, he could default to junk food at the airport or bring fruit and nuts, but the former would wreck his health and the latter had become monotonous.

Lubetzky wondered: What if he could fit the kind of nutritious whole foods he liked to eat into a more convenient package? Initially he put his hard-won experience in international business into practice and began importing healthful snack bars from an Australian company. But when the factory went bust, he had to come up with a new plan. So, he began writing out lists of possible ingredients in an attempt to re-create the imported bar. Though they would eventually be produced in a factory, for the next few months, Lubetzky and his team baked small batches, hand-cut every single bar, and packaged each individually. Believing that his product should be fully transparent in every way, Lubetzky chose to include whole nuts and fruit rather than artificial colors and flavoring, and also to use clear packaging that let potential customers see exactly what they were buying.

Now the product needed a name. His thoughts returned to the war stories his father told him when he was a boy. How could he distill his dad's life philosophy into a single word? "He taught me that even small acts of kindness—the tiniest touches of humanity—can have a transformative impact," Lubetzky told CNN.[21] So, what about *KIND Bar*? He resolved not to make philanthropy just a box check, but the very core of the company's DNA. While some slogans are catchy for their own sake, KIND's reflects its purpose to give people healthy, delicious snacks, and treat others better: "Do the KIND thing for your body, your taste buds and your world."

"The two abiding interests in my life—commerce and peacemaking—were pulling me in opposite directions," Lubetzky wrote in *Do the KIND Thing*. He resolved the dilemma by implementing what he called the "AND philosophy": do this *and* that, not this *or* that. "The way I avoided having to compromise on either of these dreams was to start my own business with a social mission."[22]

Fortunately, his experience with selling both cosmetics and food set him in good stead to build this new company, even as he continued to grow PeaceWorks. Because he had begun alone, Lubetzky had been forced to investigate just about every area of entrepreneurship himself, from sourcing to production to marketing to sales, and much more. The mistakes he made—like retaining too much stock, diversifying product lines too quickly, and mistargeting certain retail outlets—could now be used as lessons to do things better and more efficiently with KIND.

"It's important for leaders to actively look for areas where they fall short, even when they're succeeding," Lubetzky told *Fast Company*. "Celebrating lessons learned from failure not only affects your own evolution as a leader, but it also affects your culture and the way your team works and thinks. Maybe most importantly, as a leader, failures keep you grounded. They remind you that you can always do better." [23]

But to advance this mission, good intentions weren't enough. KIND needed sales. It reached a turning point in 2009, when at the urging of new investors, the company's marketing division boosted the budget of its free samples program from a paltry $800 to a whopping $800,000. This thousandfold increase was a big risk, but it paid off, as the company's revenue skyrocketed. Then came three major distribution deals with massive international retailers: Starbucks in 2009 (a contract KIND lost but later won back through sheer determination), Walmart in 2012, and Target in 2013. These partnerships led to sales doubling to 458 million bars in 2014, marking the fifth consecutive year that revenue had increased at least twofold. Lubetzky proceeded to buy back the stake owned by equity firm VMG Partners for $220 million.[24]

LEADERSHIP REFLECTIONS

· How can you apply Lubetzky's "AND philosophy" to a decision you used to frame as either/or?

· How do you plan to do things differently next time?

· Even as you succeed, what do you need to work on to be a better leader?

THREE THINGS IN LIFE ARE IMPORTANT

In keeping with KIND's determination to be "not-only-for-profit®," the company created the KIND Foundation in 2016. Its mission is to "foster kinder and more empathetic communities" by funding a wide variety of social causes. Under this umbrella, Lubetzky and his colleagues created Empatico, a multiyear, $20 million initiative to connect students around the globe. The foundation also hosts KIND Schools Challenges, which encourage middle- and high-school kids to start initiatives that benefit those in need. To date, seven recipients designated "KIND People" have received a total of $1 million to further their good works. Lubetzky also donated $25 million of his own money to get Feed the Truth off the ground. The nonprofit aims to improve health through greater transparency in the food industry.[25]

"We all have a responsibility to try and make this world better, whether it's through our work, the causes we champion, the way that we treat people, or the values we impart to the next generation," Lubetzky said after being appointed a Presidential Ambassador for Global Entrepreneurship.[26]

One of the reasons that KIND employees buy into Lubetzky's vision is because they're not merely workers, but part-owners. "Every full-time team member gets stock options and a chance to be a shareholder," Lubetzky revealed in a 2015 interview. "It's not just the financial alignment and stake, it's also a mental attitude. We really want our team members to challenge somebody to change things if something doesn't make sense."[27]

Another way that KIND takes care of its team is that nobody, Lubetzky included, will ever fire an employee unless they've committed a serious offense. "In our company, what we're trying to model is more in tune with being a family," Lubetzky said. "If we talk about things early on, 90 percent of the time issues resolve themselves. Then the person has the opportunity to grow. When there's not a fit between the skill and the need, then we try to see if the person can fit somewhere else in the company. People need to develop trust and feel comfortable that you're going to take care of each other."[28]

As well as taking good care of its employee-owners and creating its own cause-driven foundations, KIND also donates to third-party nonprofits such as City Harvest and Feeding America, with total cash investments in charitable causes exceeding $20 million. It isn't only Lubetzky, KIND, or their nonprofits that are doing good deeds, but also the company's customers. "A quarter of a million fellow kind-aholics every month receive a mission from the company to do a signature kind act," he told *Stanford Lawyer* magazine. Then the company does something even bigger to benefit the nonprofit. To date, KIND has recorded seventeen million good deeds. Customers have also logged more than three hundred thousand acts of kindness through the company's #kindawesome program.

In this way, a father telling his son about one German soldier's humanity in the midst of systemic cruelty created a ripple effect that is positively impacting hundreds of thousands of people.[29]

While Lubetzky has made more than a billion dollars, his true treasure is his family's legacy of kindness. He and his wife, Michelle, a transplant nephrologist, have four children.

"Today, our world is permeated and influenced by the private sector more than anything else," Lubetzky said when addressing Trinity University students. "Using business to advance social good, if you can figure out a way to use market forces and tackle a social challenge, it is really valuable."[30]

As KIND and its good works continue to flourish, Lubetzky's first company, PeaceWorks, is still bringing people of different backgrounds, faiths, and political views together. The brand he initially named Moshe & Ali's is now called Meditalia and is "made in cooperation between Palestinians, Israelis, Jordanians, Egyptians, Turks," he told *Forbes*. Another PeaceWorks product line sells sauces like Bali Spice, which is produced in Indonesia by Christian, Muslim, and Buddhist workers.[31] He also cofounded Maiyet, a fashion brand that supports women's collectives in developing countries. In addition, Lubetzky started OneVoice Movement, which extends the mission of PeaceWorks by amplifying the voices of moderates in Israel and Palestine who are trying to end the conflict in their region.

LEADERSHIP REFLECTIONS

· How are you helping others through your leadership?

· What can you do to inspire people to be kinder?

· What three things do you think are most important in life, and how do they guide you?

SUMMARY

In this chapter we learned that self-made billionaire Daniel Lubetzky's leadership style puts principles above profits. One of his favorite quotes is from novelist Henry James: "Three things in human life are important: The first is to be kind, the second is to be kind, and the third is to be kind." How does this work in everyday life? "Kindness is awesome because it's pure," Lubetzky explained. "When you're walking on the subway, you spot a person that has a stroller, and you help them carry it up that stairway, not only do they feel good that someone helped them, but you feel good about yourself. We call it the 'net happiness aggregator' effect of kindness—both sides are better off. We're human beings. We're sharing this planet together. Let's just be nice to one another. And when that happens, magic happens."[32]

YOUR STRONGEST ATTRIBUTE
IS A LEADERSHIP MINDSET

The good-to-great leaders never wanted to become larger-than-life heroes. They never aspired to be put on a pedestal or become unreachable icons. They were seemingly ordinary people quietly producing extraordinary results.

—JIM COLLINS, *author of* Good to Great

Leaders come to us from many walks of life and make an impact on society and others in myriad ways. Yet, though someone may have the best teammates, the latest high-tech equipment, or access to the best resources, that person might not necessarily be a leader. Some people choose to be leaders, while others are placed into leadership roles due to circumstance. Whether one is making the choice to lead or being placed in a position to lead, there must be leadership equity to pull from. This equity is a mental savings account that has accumulated a broad body of experiences, a set of core driving principles, and muscle memory to draw upon when needed.

Nick Peters of the District Fire Management office drew upon a key Stoic principle that emphasizes transformative communication. This is an important addition to the leadership toolbox. If you can't communicate your ideas or listen to others, there is little hope for effective collaboration or support from the bench. In managing his crew of firefighters,

Peters emphasized the importance of drawing dialogue back to policies and procedures that reflected fire management values of duty, integrity, and respect. If a conversation got heated or sidetracked, he redirected attention back to his department's fundamental tenets.

Another Stoic principle Peters applied was the concept of putting energy only into what can be controlled. Obviously, this is vital in fighting natural fires, which are invariably unpredictable. This same kind of mindset was apparent when Tammie Jo Shults needed to land a plane calmly and safely after an uncontained engine failure. In her early training and through supportive mentors, she learned that, although one needs to listen, it is not helpful to be reactionary. A leader needs to take in all the information, calmly think about it, and decide what action to take. It wouldn't be much good to have a flight captain yelling, panicking, and berating a crew as a plane plummets to the ground.

The ability to take in, absorb, and process information means being sociable. Good leaders are not isolated at the top, nor are they making unilateral decisions from a lofty command post. Although history books may center on a famous general or a notable emperor, in fact, real leaders on the ground are very much tuned in to their crew, supporters, and teams. For example, Shults took an interest in her crew each and every flight, which gave her the situational awareness to trust that her crew would do what was necessary when she had to concentrate on piloting Flight 1380 to a safe landing.

Similarly, neurosurgeon Katrina Firlik learned early on from Peter Jannetta that, for leaders to gain respect, they need to support their team. When a patient asked Dr. Jannetta not to have any residents "training-in" on the surgery, he responded: "Our stellar success rates are based on our team approach. And I quote you that because that's what we do in every case. And we don't make exceptions. If we made exceptions, I don't know what our success rate would be." We follow leaders who have our back.

Along with the day-to-day actions of a leader, there are also those moments when a crisis or key decision necessitates simply that: a decision. It is in those times that a leader emerges valiantly rather than just being a figurehead who crumbles. This ability involves a very imaginative, contemplative, and reflective mindset. Such training can come from hundreds, if not thousands, of hours, behind the controls of a plane and in simulator training. Elite athletes practice more than weekend warriors, with some suggesting ten thousand hours as the minimum threshold for mastery. Surgeons spend considerable time planning an operation, deliberating the approach, considering possible options, and then quieting their minds before entering the operating room.

As Paul Ratcliffe emphasized, leaders also nurture and support a particular culture. Culture is emphasized by all of the leaders we've met in the preceding pages, whether it was feeling the ability to speak freely about anything on Tammie Jo Shults's flight or Katrina Firlik's choice not to yell and scream at her scrub nurses and instead calmly communicate what she required during a procedure. Few great accomplishments are the work of solely one person. Instead, it is the particular human ability to work with other humans to create a larger, more powerful "entity" that allows us to fly airplanes, fight wildfires, win World Cups, and more.

Each of the leaders whose stories are shared in this book also recognize that their leadership doesn't exist for its own sake or merely to further their personal aims. Rather, their role is that of a servant-leader who guides others to rally around and achieve a higher common purpose. For Nic Gill, this is preparing the New Zealand All Blacks to play every game in a way that honors the legacy of their famous black jersey. In the case of Steve Kerr, it's employing the Core Four values of joy, mindfulness, compassion, and competition in everything that the Golden State Warriors do to propel them not just to win, but to win the right way. And for Daniel Lubetzky, his entire life's work has been about creating businesses that bridge gaps, bringing people of different races, colors, and creeds together, and, as he puts it, "Using business to advance social good."

Last, all our leaders talk about finding balance in life. Nick Peters emphasized this when he noted that family time allows him to put aside the stress of his work for some moments to regroup and reenergize. At the end of the day, the Stoics were certainly on point when they said that "human nature is inherently social. We have a bond of natural affection toward our children and loved ones." Leaders are adept at bringing out the best in a group of people, whether it's at work, at home, or further afield. This alludes to the true gift of cultivating a Leader's Mind. Doing so won't merely help you overcome hardships, tame career transitions, and meet your own goals, it will also enable you to guide, develop, and empower others to make a positive difference in their lives, communities, and the wider world.

THE LEADERSHIP PLEDGE

I demonstrate leadership by:

- Talking with and listening to my team, colleagues, and clients.
- Engaging in positive communication to build trust and collaboration.
- Being there day in and day out, and being professional in all aspects.
- Committing to get better every day, and empowering my team to do the same.
- Modeling core values in everything I do.
- Embracing challenges as opportunities to learn and grow.
- Finding ways to serve people selflessly and humbly.
- Identifying a higher purpose and using it as fuel to chase excellence in everything.
- Forging a leadership legacy by mentoring others.
- Creating and nurturing a balanced life.

ACKNOWLEDGMENTS

FROM JIM AFREMOW

Once again, I have been blessed with many special people to thank.

To my superstar wife, Anne, and our wonderful daughter, Maria Paz, for lovingly supporting and inspiring me during the time and duties that this book required.

To Phil White for being a true leader and a five-star teammate on this project. Your interviewing skills and writing abilities are truly world-class. Thanks a million for making the entire process such a blast.

To my incredible literary agent, Helen Adams, who championed this project every step of the way. You have a special knack for providing the right guidance in the right way at the right time, every time.

To the championship-caliber team at HarperCollins Leadership for their expertise and thoughtfulness, and for making this project really shine, all the way from conception to cover design to marketing. Specific thanks to our superb editor, Sara Kendrick, and her unbeatable team—Jeff Farr, Beth Metrick, Zoe Kaplan, Aryn Van Dyke, Brittany Prescott, and Tim Burgard.

Every person interviewed in this book—Nick Peters, Tammie Jo Shults, Nic Gill, Katrina Firlik, Paul Ratcliffe, and Donald Robertson—generously contributed hours of their time and provided candid recollections about how they have prepared, performed, and prevailed in their leadership roles. We are in their debt.

FROM PHIL WHITE

I'd like to thank my wife, Nicole, for editing the earliest version of this book and for her continued inspiration in writing, love, and life. People see the end result of words on a page but not the tireless hours she puts into making my waffling vaguely readable. My sons, Johnny and Harry, did a great job of keeping quiet while Jim and I were interviewing the leaders featured in this book and with adding fun into the mix when the words started to blur on the screen. My family and friends kept me going with a mixture of encouragement and support. It's a privilege to team up with a coauthor as knowledgeable, enthusiastic, and kind as Jim, who is the perfect creative partner. We might've been able to interview some of these great leaders by ourselves, but to do so together and have someone to geek out with afterward was a true pleasure.

Speaking of our interviewees, I'd like to thank Gilly, Tammie Jo, Katrina, Nick, Paul, and Donald for taking the time to share their expertise. The same goes to Daniel Lubetzky and Steve Kerr for serving as inspirations to me and many others. This book would never have come together without the stellar efforts of our agent, Helen Adams, or the vision of our editor, Sara Kendrick. I'd also like to acknowledge the help of Aryn Van Dyke and her colleague Brittany, Tim Burgard, Jeff Farr, Beth Metrick, Zoe Kaplan, and the entire HarperCollins Leadership team in making *The Leader's Mind* look and read better. Finally, I give credit to God—the ultimate leader—for the blessing of making a living telling stories.

ENDNOTES

Introduction

1. Jamie Pandaram, "Are the All Blacks the Greatest International Team in the History of Sport?" *Daily Telegraph*, October 23, 2016, available online at https://www.dailytelegraph.com.au/sport/rugby/are-the-all-blacks -the-greatest-international-team-in-the-history-of-sport/news-story /f61ad2d65623a9586929bbfba386b157.

Chapter 1: Leadership under fire

1. F. Capozzi, C. Beyan, A. Pierro, A. Koul, V. Murino, S. Livi, A. P. Bayliss, J. Ristic, C. Becchio, "Tracking The Leader: Gaze Behavior in Group Interactions," *ISCIENCE*, Vol. 16, 242–249, June 28, 2019, https:// doi.org/10.1016/j.isci.2019.05.035.
2. Author's interview with Nick Peters, December 13, 2019.

Chapter 2: The Sharpshooter

1. James Herbert, "Landing a Punch on Michael Jordan," ESPN, September 23, 2013, https://www.espn.com/blog/truehoop/post/_ /id/61933/landing-a-punch-on-michael-jordan.
2. Herbert, "Landing a Punch."
3. Chris Ballard, *The Art of the Beautiful Game: The Thinking Fan's Tour of the NBA* (New York: Simon & Schuster, 2009), 37.
4. Aaron Dodson, "On This Day in NBA Finals History: Steve Kerr's 17-Foot Jumper Clinches Bulls' 1997 Title," The Undefeated, June 13, 2017, https://theundefeated.com/features/nba -finals-history-steve-kerr-17-foot-jumper-clinches-bulls-1997-title/.
5. Melissa Rohlin, "Steve Kerr and Gregg Popovich Open Up About Their Relationship," *Mercury News*, March 7, 2018, https:// www.mercurynews.com/2018/03/07/gregg-popovich-and-steve -kerr-open-up-about-their-relationship/.
6. Rohlin, "Steve Kerr and Gregg Popovich."

7. Rohlin, "Steve Kerr and Gregg Popovich."

8. Chris Ballard, "Warriors: From One-Dimensional and One-and-Done to NBA Title Favorites," *Sports Illustrated*, February 18, 2015, https://www.si.com/nba/2015/02/20/golden-state-warriors-steve-kerr-stephen-curry-klay-thompson-joe-lacob.

9. Nick Schwartz, "Steve Kerr Will Make an Insane Amount of Money as a First-Time Coach," *USA Today*, May 14, 2014, https://ftw.usatoday.com/2014/05/steve-kerr-knicks-warriors-coach-money.

10. Ballard, "Warriors: From One-Dimensional and One-and-Done to NBA Title Favorites."

11. Michael Gervais, "Steve Kerr, Golden State Warriors Head Coach," *Finding Mastery*, January 23, 2019, https://findingmastery.net/steve-kerr/.

12 Tim Kawakami, "Luke Walton, Steve Kerr and the Warriors' Four Core Values: Joy, Mindfulness, Compassion and Competition," *Mercury News*, November 24, 2015, http://blogs.mercurynews.com/kawakami/2015/11/24/luke-walton-steve-kerr-and-the-warriors-four-core-values-joy-mindfulness-compassion-and-competition/.

13. "Steve Kerr's 4 Core Values: Joy, Mindfulness, Compassion, Competition," Positive Coaching Alliance, https://devzone.positivecoach.org/resource/audio/steve-kerrs-4-core-values-joy-mindfulness-compassion-competition.

14. "Leadership Lessons from Steve Kerr, Head Coach of the Golden State Warriors," *Open View Partners*, June 13, 2017, https://openviewpartners.com/blog/leadership-lessons-from-steve-kerr/#.XZQAlEZKjD4.

15. Baxter Holmes, "The Charcuterie Board That Revolutionized Basketball," *ESPN the Magazine*, October 11, 2017, http://www.espn.com/espn/feature/story/_/page/enterpriseWarriors/how-steve-kerr-revolutionized-golden-state-warriors-offense-charcuterie-board.

16. K. C. Johnson, "Former Bulls Assistant Ron Adams Is the 'Truth Teller' on Steve Kerr's Warriors Staff," *Chicago Tribune*, June 2, 2018, https://www.chicagotribune.com/sports/bulls/ct-spt-warriors-ron-adams-nba-finals-20180602-story.html.

17. Ballard, "Warriors: From One-Dimensional and One-and-Done to NBA Title Favorites."

18. Kit Rachlis, "The Road to Destiny," *California Sunday Magazine*, September 19, 2018, https://story.californiasunday.com/steve-kerr-phil-jackson.

19. Baxter Holmes, "Special Force at Work for Warriors," ESPN, June 5, 2015, https://www.espn.com/nba/playoffs/2015/story/_/id/13022401/nba-playoffs-special-forces-working-warriors.

20. Tim Kawakami, "A Warriors Bond Across the Decades: The 1975 Title Team Was about 'Togetherness,' For the Current Group It's 'Just Us,'" *Mercury News*, March 24, 2015, http://blogs.mercurynews.com /kawakami/2015/03/24/togetherness-just-us-xxxx/.

21. Mackey Craven, "Leadership Lessons from Steve Kerr, Head Coach of the Golden State Warriors," *Open View Partners*.

22. Rachel Bachman and Ben Cohen, "The Medical Riddle of Steve Kerr's Back Pain," *Wall Street Journal*, May 13, 2017, https://www.wsj.com /articles/the-medical-riddle-of-steve-kerrs-back-pain-1494673201.

23. "Steve Kerr, Golden State Warriors Head Coach," *Finding Mastery*.

24. Joe Vardon, "'Re-Imagine Everything and Adapt': Steve Kerr Has a New Warriors Mentality," *The Athletic*, September 11, 2019, https:// theathletic.com/1196717/2019/09/11/re-imagine-everything-and-adapt-steve-kerr-has-a-new-warriors-mentality/.

25. Vardon, "'Re-Imagine Everything."

26. Wes Goldberg, "Steve Kerr on Klay Thompson's Injury, Kelly Oubre's Fit and the Warriors Getting Back 'In the Mix,'" *Mercury News*, November 25, 2020, https://www.mercurynews.com/2020/11/25 /steve-kerr-on-klay-thompsons-injury-kelly-oubres-fit-and-the-warriors -getting-in-the-mix/.

27. Ethan Strauss, "'It's More About Efficiency and Process': Steve Kerr is Learning From Gregg Popovich and the World With Team USA," *The Athletic*, September 12, 2019, available online at https://theathletic .com/1205317/2019/09/12/its-more-about-efficiency-and-process -steve-kerr-is-learning-from-gregg-popovich-and-the-world-with -team-usa/.

28. "Already a World Cup Champion, USA Assistant Coach Steve Kerr Looking for Second Title in China," FIBA, September 6, 2019, http:// www.fiba.basketball/basketballworldcup/2019/news/already-a -world-cup-champion-usa-assistant-coach-steve-kerr-looking-for- second-title-in-china.

29. *Flying Coach* with Steve Kerr & Pete Carroll, episode one, https:// www.theringer.com/2020/4/13/21218869/flying-coach-with-steve -kerr-pete-carroll-two-champions-mentors-philosophies-why-they -coach-premiere.

30 *Flying Coach* with Steve Kerr & Pete Carroll, episode one.

31. *Flying Coach* with Steve Kerr & Pete Carroll, episode one.

32. *Flying Coach* with Steve Kerr & Pete Carroll, episode one.

33. *Flying Coach* with Steve Kerr & Pete Carroll, episode one.

Chapter 3: Grace Under Pressure

1. Richard Goldstein, "Rosemary Mariner, Pathbreaking Navy Pilot and Commander, Is Dead at 65," *New York Times*, February 1, 2019, https://www.nytimes.com/2019/02/01/obituaries/rosemary-mariner-dead.html.
2. Karen Dunlap, "In Memoriam: Rosemary Mariner," University of Tennessee, Knoxville News, January 29, 2019, https://news.utk.edu/2019/01/29/in-memoriam-rosemary-mariner/.

Chapter 4: The Man in Black

1. "All or Nothing: New Zealand All Blacks," 2018, available online at https://www.amazon.com/All-Nothing-Zealand-Blacks-Season/dp/B07DF6KWC6.
2. Staff profile, University of Waikato, https://www.waikato.ac.nz/staff-profiles/people/ngill.

Chapter 5: On the Cutting Edge

1. "About Katrina Firlik," HealthPrize Technologies, http://katrinafirlik.com/katrina-firlik/.

Chapter 6: Shaping Future Leaders

1. "Women's Soccer," Stanford University, https://gostanford.com/sports/womens-soccer/roster/coaches/paul-ratcliffe/3614.

Chapter 7: Lead Like a Roman Emperor

1. Condensed and referencing an "Introduction to Stoicism" by Donald Robertson, at the opening of the Modern Stoicism Conference, Stoicon 2017, held in Toronto, Canada.
2. "Introduction to Stoicism" by Donald Robertson.
3. "Introduction to Stoicism" by Donald Robertson.
4. "Introduction to Stoicism" by Donald Robertson.
5. "Introduction to Stoicism" by Donald Robertson.
6. "Introduction to Stoicism" by Donald Robertson.

Chapter 8: The Leader's Mission

1. Interview with Daniel Lubetzky, LinkedIn Speaker Series, December 10, 2015, https://www.youtube.com/watch?v=l9JyudPe7mA.
2. Rich Tenorio, "These US Soldiers Liberated Dachau While Their Own Families Were Locked Up Back Home," *Times of Israel,* May 29, 2017, https://www.timesofisrael.com/these-us-soldiers-liberated-dachau-while-their-own-families-were-locked-up-back-home/; "This Day in History: US Army Liberates Dachau Concentration Camp," History.com, July 28, 2019, https://www.history.com/this-day-in-history/dachau-liberated.
3. Daniel Lubetzky, "5 Lessons from My Father, for My Kids," CNN, June 19, 2015, https://www.cnn.com/2015/06/19/opinions/lubetzky-fathers-day/index.html.
4. Lubetzky, "5 Lessons."
5. Marc Peruzzi, "Do the Kind Thing," *First Descents,* publication date unknown, https://firstdescents.org/do-the-kind-thing-2/.
6. Daniel Lubetzky, "5 Lessons from My Father, for My Kids," CNN, June 19, 2015, https://www.cnn.com/2015/06/19/opinions/lubetzky-fathers-day/index.html.
7. Daniel Lubetzky, *Do the KIND Thing: Think Boundlessly, Work Purposefully, Live Passionately* (New York: Ballantine Books, 2015), 68.
8. Lubetzky, *Do the KIND Thing,* 69.
9. Lubetzky, 71–72.
10. Jeremy Gerlach, "A New Kind of Entrepreneur," Trinity University, March 15, 2019, https://new.trinity.edu/news/new-kind-entrepreneur.
11. Daniel Lubetzky, *Do the KIND Thing: Think Boundlessly, Work Purposefully, Live Passionately* (New York: Ballantine Books, 2015), 78.
12. Lubetzky, *Do the KIND Thing,* 25.
13. Lindsay Lavine, "The Many Mistakes That Led To KIND Snacks' Success," *Fast Company,* February 17, 2015, https://www.fastcompany.com/3042380/the-many-mistakes-the-led-to-kind-snacks-success.
14. Daniel Lubetzky, *Do the KIND Thing: Think Boundlessly, Work Purposefully, Live Passionately* (New York: Ballantine Books, 2015, 30.
15. Interview with Daniel Lubetzky, LinkedIn Speaker Series, December 10, 2015, https://www.youtube.com/watch?v=l9JyudPe7mA.
16. Daniel Lubetzky, *Do the KIND Thing: Think Boundlessly, Work Purposefully, Live Passionately* (New York: Ballantine Books, 2015, 33.
17. Sharon Driscoll, "Peace, Kindness, and Understanding—and Snacks," *Stanford Lawyer,* November 11, 2013, https://

law.stanford.edu/stanford-lawyer/articles/peace-kindness
-and-%E2%80%A8understanding-and-snacks/.

18. Daniel Lubetzky, *Do the KIND Thing: Think Boundlessly, Work Purposefully, Live Passionately* (New York: Ballantine Books, 2015, 68.

19. Daniel Lubetzky, *Do the KIND Thing*, 61–63.

20. Carolyn Sun, "5 Business Lessons from KIND Founder and CEO Daniel Lubetzky," October 7, 2015, *Entrepreneur*, https://www.entrepreneur.com/article/251438.

21. Daniel Lubetzky, "5 Lessons from My Father, for My Kids," CNN, June 19, 2015, https://www.cnn.com/2015/06/19/opinions/lubetzky-fathers-day/index.html.

22. Daniel Lubetzky, *Do the KIND Thing: Think Boundlessly, Work Purposefully, Live Passionately* (New York: Ballantine Books, 2015, 78.

23. Lavine, "The Many Mistakes That Led To KIND Snacks' Success."

24. Gabe Friedman, "How a Holocaust Legacy Helped Launch the Kind Bar Brand," *Jewish Telegraphic Agency*, October 22, 2015, https://www.jta.org/2015/10/22/united-states/how-a-holocaust-legacy-helped-launch-the-kind-bar-brand; Shasha Dai, "KIND Reunites with Founder as Private-Equity Firm Cashes Out," *Wall Street Journal*, March 6, 2014, https://blogs.wsj.com/moneybeat/2014/03/06/kind-reunites-with-founder-as-private-equity-firm-cashes-out/.

25. "Get to Know Our Founder," KIND, https://www.kindsnacks.com/about-us.html; "The KIND Foundation," KIND, https://www.kindsnacks.com/foundation.html.

26. Daniel Lubetzky, "5 Lessons from My Father, for My Kids," CNN, June 19, 2015, https://www.cnn.com/2015/06/19/opinions/lubetzky-fathers-day/index.html.

27. Interview with Daniel Lubetzky, LinkedIn Speaker Series, December 10, 2015, https://www.youtube.com/watch?v=l9JyudPe7mA.

28. Interview with Daniel Lubetzky.

29. Driscoll, "Peace, Kindness, and Understanding—and Snacks."

30. Gerlach, "A New Kind of Entrepreneur."

31. Nina Roberts, "What Drives Social Entrepreneurs? A Q&A with Daniel Lubetzky, Founder and CEO of Kind Snacks," *Forbes*, November 27, 2017, https://www.forbes.com/sites/ninaroberts/2017/11/27/what-drives-social-entrepreneurs-a-qa-with-daniel-lubetzky-founder-and-ceo-of-kind-snacks/#59a041c12e89.

32. Interview with Daniel Lubetzky, LinkedIn Speaker Series, December 10, 2015, https://www.youtube.com/watch?v=l9JyudPe7mA.

INDEX

ABOUT THE AUTHORS

Dr. Jim Afremow is a much sought-after mental skills coach, licensed professional counselor, cocreator of the Champion's Mind app, and the author of *The Champion's Mind: How Great Athletes Think, Train and Thrive* (Rodale, 2014), *The Champion's Comeback: How Great Athletes Recover, Reflect, and Reignite* (Rodale, 2016), and *The Young Champion's Mind: How to Think, Train, and Thrive Like an Elite Athlete* (Rodale, 2018).

Though his practice is located in Eugene, Oregon, Jim provides individual and group mental skills training and leadership services across the globe to athletes, teams, and coaches in all sports, as well as to parents, business professionals, and all others engaged in highly demanding endeavors. He is passionate about helping others achieve peak performance and personal excellence, and live a gold medal life.

For more than twenty-five years, Jim has assisted numerous high school, collegiate, and professional athletes and coaches. Major sports organizations represented include MLB, NBA, WNBA, PGA Tour, LPGA Tour, NHL, NFL, and the UFC. In addition, he has worked closely with scores of US and international Olympians. He served as the staff mental coach for two international Olympic teams, the Greek Olympic softball team and India's Olympic field hockey team. He served as a senior staff member with Counseling

Services at Arizona State University and as the peak performance coordinator with the San Francisco Giants MLB
organization.

Jim resides in Eugene with his wife, Anne, and their
daughter, Maria Paz. He loves spending time with his family and hitting a little white ball around a field.

Keep in touch with Jim via the web:

Website: https://www.goldmedalmind.net/

Twitter: http://www.twitter.com/goldmedalmind

Instagram: https://instagram.com/jimafremow/

Phil White has been writing stories for as long as he can
remember. Among his fourteen books, he is the coauthor
of *Waterman 2.0* with Kelly Starrett, *The 17 Hour Fast* with
Dr. Frank Merritt, *Unplugged* with Andy Galpin and Brian
Mackenzie, *Game Changer* with Fergus Connolly, and *The
Align Method* with Aaron Alexander. Phil received an Emmy
nomination for his Kansas City history collaboration with
award-winning director Greg Sheffer. As well as writing
books together, he and Jim Afremow have teamed up with
entrepreneur Dave Kearney to create The Champion's Mind
app, which is used by pro, college, high school, and club
teams across the globe.

Phil also collaborates with a select group of high-
performance brands, including Momentous, TD Athletes
Edge, Fusion Sport, and TrainingPeaks. In a previous life,
he wrote *A Lion in the Heartland,* which tells the story of
how Winston Churchill ended up in the middle of Missouri
to deliver his Iron Curtain Speech, and *Whistle Stop,* which
chronicles the unlikely comeback of President Harry Truman in the 1948 election. When not writing, Phil can be

found hiking and paddleboarding with his wife and editor, Nicole (who is also a fashion designer), and his two sons/budding filmmakers, Johnny and Harry, in the wilds of Colorado.

Follow Phil on Instagram @philwhitebooks and keep up with his books, podcasts, and articles at philwhitebooks.com and https://www.clippings.me/philwhitebooks.

Listen to Jim and Phil's podcast at championconversationspodcast.com, where you can also subscribe to their newsletter.